Nose Jobs For Peace

Nose Jobs For Peace

by

Selma Diamond

Prentice-Hall, Inc.,
Englewood Cliffs, N.J.

ISBN 0-13-623827-0
Library of Congress Catalog Card Number: 71-115834

Printed in the United States of America   T

Prentice-Hall International, Inc., London
Prentice-Hall of Australia, Pty. Ltd., Sydney
Prentice-Hall of Canada, Ltd., Toronto
Prentice-Hall of India Private Ltd., New Delhi
Prentice-Hall of Japan, Inc., Tokyo

Acknowledgment is made for the use of the article
"Say What You Want About Doctors," © 1966 The Hearst
Corporation.

CONTENTS

Nose Jobs For Peace

One

TV & Me

You know what a lot of people ask me? If my life as a TV writer has been affected by my appearances on television.

It certainly has—and I'm enjoying it except for one thing. It's costing me money. I've got to tip more.

There's a place in my neighborhood where I always have my breakfast. Well, until I started appearing on television, as far as the counterman was concerned, I was just another customer ordering orange juice and chow mein. Now I'm "Miss Diamond" ordering orange juice and chow mein. Well, you can't leave a twenty-cent tip when you're getting personalized service . . . so right away there's another nickel added to the tip.

And on the bus it costs me more now.

Like, one morning I got on the bus holding a quarter and the bus driver said to me, "Aren't you Selma Diamond?"

I got so excited I dropped the quarter into the coin box.

So I said to the bus driver, "I just dropped a quarter into the coin box. You have to give me a nickel change."

So he said to me, "I can't do that. The quarter's been registered on the machine. You'll have to wait until another passenger gets on with nickels and I'll give you one."

Well, I sat on that bus for block after block and everybody who got on had their exact fare in dimes. Finally I decided to take my nickel loss and get off the bus because I was miles from my stop.

Taking a cab back to where I was supposed to get off ran into money, too. I had to give the cab driver a bigger tip than I usually do because he asked me for my autograph. In less than an hour I blew one dollar and thirty cents.

Another thing that costs me money now is going to a beauty parlor to have my hair cut. I used to cut my own hair. What difference did it make if it didn't always come out the same? Nobody ever notices a writer's hair. Well, I can't do that now. On television they notice it.

And another thing that's happened is that when I walk along the street, some people greet me by my first name. It's a little odd but I suppose I'll get used to it just like others who are identified by just one name. You know, Picasso, Garbo, Drāno.

The most gratifying experience of all this is that now I get respect from my butcher. This is no small achievement, considering the fact that he gets no big holiday orders from me. Holidays I'm invited to join friends, so he's doing no big turkey, leg of lamb, or rib roast business with me.

With all his respect going to his customers who have twelve over for a sit-down dinner, you can't expect him to respect half a pound of ground chuck.

But now when I go in for that half a pound of ground chuck, he not only grinds it to order but gives me all the free parsley I want.

❧ They Don't Know Me In Trieste

I have a friend who won a shoe factory in Trieste in a crap game. It was during World War II. He won it from a fellow who had put up the bomber he was flying against the bomber my friend was flying.

When it came time to pay off, the other fellow didn't have a bill of sale for the bomber so my friend took the shoe factory instead for which the other fellow did have proof of ownership.

After the war my friend went to Trieste. He lives there now but every once in a while he comes back to the United States for a few days on shoe business. When he does, he usually calls me and we have dinner.

He knows I'm a television writer but since he sees no American television in Trieste and he's never here long enough to become a watcher, I've never mentioned to him that I appear on TV.

I guess it's because when I'm out with a fellow I don't talk about myself, I let him talk. I force myself— but I let him talk.

Most of the time I find what people have to tell me interesting and if it isn't interesting I act as if it's interesting. It's either that or eating an awful lot of dinners alone.

No harm is done because it never occurs to a man that what he's saying isn't interesting. After all, he's a man . . . so he's interesting. Heaven knows, we tell him often enough.

Please, I'm not knocking this. It's the game men and women play and still the best game in town. He's Mr. Interesting and I'm Miss Lucky to be having dinner with an interesting man.

So anyway, I'm having dinner with my friend and he's telling me some interesting stories about running a shoe factory in Trieste.

While we're sitting there, people who recognize me come over to talk. One nice lady came over to tell me about her wonderful cure for hives. She had seen me and heard me talk about my terrible hives on the Carson Show. Then another woman came over with her remedy for hives. Several other people stopped by to mention that I ought to do something about my hair . . . or to ask the name of my hairdresser. The owner of a pet shop came over, left his card and suggested I drop by his shop and buy an anteater to give me "style."

Suddenly my friend gets up and excuses himself. I continued eating.

I didn't panic that he didn't come back right away.

Five minutes passed, then ten minutes . . . I got to thinking the check'll come and he's not here.

I decided the best thing for me to do is to finish the dinner because I can always face disaster better on a full stomach.

Right after I decided this, he came back.

I said to him, "Where have you been? You've been gone such a long time."

So he says, "We're sitting here and perfect strangers come over, people whom you obviously have never met . . . yet they're talking to you and recognizing you. So I went to the men's room, gave the attendant a dollar and asked him who you are."

So now I started telling him about the Tonight Show and Johnny Carson and explained that being on the show is what has made me so recognizable.

Then he gave me a dollar and said, "Who's Johnny Carson?"

After I took the dollar, I told him that for a couple more dollars I'd tell him about Virginia Graham, Merv Griffin, Mike Douglas, Joey Bishop, Steve Allen, Dick Cavett, Dennis Wholley and David Frost.

He acted like it was interesting.

Some Strangers Are Very Strange

One day, just as I was leaving NBC from the Sixth Avenue side, a fellow comes rushing toward me from out of Hurley's Bar.

Since the AFTRA strike, to me, Hurley's is the Sixth Avenue entrance to the Twilight Zone.

It was at Hurley's that we picked up our strike placards. There was a warm welcome of hot coffee and sandwiches for the pickets and it was here that the latest news of the negotiations between the major networks and AFTRA was exchanged.

I'll never forget the feeling I got in there. It was like

AFTRA was Sinn Fein. The year was 1916. I was an Irish Nationalist. It was in Hurley's that the Easter Rebellion was planned. And that autographed glossy of Jack Paar in Hurley's window wasn't Jack Paar at all, but Eamon de Valera.

So when this fellow comes rushing toward me out of Hurley's and gives me a big "Hello, Selma," even though I didn't remember ever seeing him before in this life, I figured since he knows me, maybe I met him in one of my other lives.

Then he said, "You have no idea how glad I am to see you. C'mon and let me buy you a drink."

While he was talking I kept looking at him for some kind of hint as to who he was. I noticed he was wearing a wedding ring.

I said, "Thank you, no."

One thing I'm sure of, no matter how many lives I have lived before, in the one I'm living now I've never wasted time having a drink with a married man. First of all, where is it going to get you! And besides, I'm chicken.

Then he says to me, "I've got to talk to you. I have a big problem and you're one of the few women I know who makes sense."

Now, when a fellow tells you, "you make sense," believe me, you're not the girl of his dreams, and even if you get looped with him, you are unflatteringly safe.

I certainly don't need this, so I said, "I really am in a rush."

Well, you never saw such a sad, hurt-little-boy look that came over his face as he said, "Please, Selma."

I fell right into the trap as any woman is trapped when a man gets that sad, hurt-little-boy look on his face. Even though you haven't done anything to put that look on his face, you immediately assume the burden of the woman who did put it there.

Right away you want to do something for him to make the hurt better . . . like find him an ouchless bandage, warm a glass of milk for him, rub his chest with Vick's and promise never to do again whatever it was you never did to him.

"Okay," I said. "Let's have a cup of coffee."

While all this is going on I'm still trying to figure out where I know him from.

As we're having our coffee, he's telling me his problems.

His wife is cold to him. He's so unhappy about this, it's affecting his work and he thinks he's going to lose his job.

His daughter has begun to stay out all night and won't tell him where she's been.

His son is running around with a crowd that makes it impossible to keep bananas around the house.

All the time he's talking about his problems I'm thinking, "What am I doing here? I don't watch Peyton Place and suddenly I'm in it!"

What's more, I'm beginning to think I have never met this man before. Nobody I know tells me their problems. They have an analyst.

Just as he was telling me how his father-in-law turned him down for a loan to pay his daughter's orthodontist something on account so as not to interrupt the work on her overbite, I said, "Pardon me, but where did we first meet?"

He said, "We never met."

I got real mad and I said, "You've got your nerve putting me in this pretty embarrassing situation."

"What about me?" he says. "How do you think I felt sitting here when I realized I didn't know you either."

"But you called me by name," I said. "When you came over to me in the street."

"I know," he said. "And I'm sorry. The only way I can explain it is that I see you on television and when I saw you in front of Hurley's you looked so familiar to me I thought you were somebody I knew."

I didn't stay mad at him but I didn't stay either.

I can understand this happening because it once happened to me.

It was my first day in Hollywood. I didn't know anybody. Wherever I walked all I saw were strangers. I walked all the way to Beverly Hills from Hollywood Boulevard and right on to Beverly Drive.

I finally saw a familiar face. I ran right over to him and said, "What're you doing in Hollywood?"

He smiled, got into his car and drove on.

Nobody had a better right to be in Hollywood. It was Cary Grant.

𝕬 I'm Elizabeth Taylor
In Cincinnati

I had never been to San Francisco until Gypsy Rose Lee invited me to come up and chat with her on her show.

When I got to San Francisco it really knocked me out. Here's a city that really keeps its cool.

I watched the people jumping on and off moving cable cars and treating each other to Rice-a-Roni like there had never been the San Francisco fire, earthquake or the Republican convention that nominated Barry Goldwater for President.

They have rebuilt after every disaster and the city is as modern and new as any city in the country with as many hills.

You look at San Francisco and then you look at Rome with its hills and believe me, those Italians should take lessons from San Francisco on how to keep up a city.

Did you ever see how the Italians have let the Pantheon run down. They tell you the Pantheon was built in 27 B.C. Even if they didn't tell you, from the condition it's in, you could guess.

You'll never see the Cow Palace neglected like that.

And the people who recognized me from TV came over and talked to me as they do in most cities I visit. And, as in most cities, some of the people who recognized me didn't always remember my name or my face.

What they recognized was a face from TV and not necessarily mine. They just point at me and say "Hermione Gingold," "Dick Cavett," "Shirley Booth," "Ed Sullivan."

So when they ask me for my autograph I write whatever name they call out.

Why not? They never look to see what I'm writing and I'm sure they'd rather have the autograph of the person they thought I was anyway.

Something like this happened while I was in Magnin's.

The dress department was rather crowded and my salesgirl asked me if I minded sharing a fitting room. I didn't, so I did.

And sure enough, the lady I was sharing the fitting room with recognized me, but didn't remember my name, and pointed at me saying, "Johnny Carson."

So when she asked for my autograph, I signed "Johnny Carson."

Like I said, she didn't look, just folded it up and put it in her bag.

Then she said to me, "Oh, is my husband going to be

surprised when I get home and show him whose autograph I got."

I was thinking: Is she going to be surprised when she
gets home and shows him whose autograph she got and
her husband says to her, "Where did you get Johnny
Carson's autograph?"

And she says, "We shared the same fitting room in
Magnin's."

Two

Who Says You Can't Go Home Again?

When I was out in Hollywood writing, I made a little money and achieved a certain dignified obscurity. So on my first visit back to New York, you know how it is, you've got to visit the old neighborhood and "show them."

I wanted to show them I was wearing classy Hollywood clothes. I didn't have to shop in Klein's basement anymore. I could shop in Klein's Annex. I could go to Orbach's Oval Room and buy an original copy of a Paris original.

What's more, if I wanted to make myself a dress, I didn't have to go bargain hunting in remnant stores. I could walk into Gimbels' yardage department and buy the exact yardage the dress pattern suggested. No longer did I need to face the bitter challenge of maneuvering a dress pattern my size on a remnant that would be a challenge if I were two sizes smaller.

So I decided to go around to Kings Highway, where I used to live and impress the person I impressed the least when I was a child, the candy-store man.

I walked into the candy store after being away for nine years and sure enough, there was Mr. Landsman, the candy-store man.

The phone in the phone booth was ringing. The phone in the phone booth was always ringing, because in my neighborhood, as in most New York City neighborhoods, even though you didn't have a phone, you had a phone number. You gave it to your friends and told them, "The phone is in the candy store, the candy-store man will call me."

Mr. Landsman hustled his bulk into the phone booth. Picking up the receiver and not even waiting to hear who was calling, or for whom, he said, "I'm alone in the store. I've got nobody to send."

There was a slight pause and then I heard him say, "Okay, if you want to wait, wait."

This was often foolishly interpreted by the person on the other end as capitulation and just as often they were foolishly wrong.

When Mr. Landsman left the phone booth with the

receiver swinging off the hook and repeating, "Okay, if you want to wait, wait," it was just to let some time pass before he came back to say, "Nobody is home there" and hang up before he became further committed.

This was not his constant attitude toward telephone callers. If the caller or callee were customers, Mr. Landsman could always find somebody to "send." There were always three children of his own hanging around the store and children hanging around his children.

When your friend's father owns a candy store, the rewards of your loyalty and love include fringe benefits that could not be bought with pure gold. These benefits are a Comstock Lode of melting ice cream when the freezing unit breaks down, you share the secret of how to get Indian nuts out of the penny machine without putting in any pennies, you're there when the candy-store man makes a double double rich chocolate malted milk for his child and his child never drinks alone.

Somehow I expected Mr. Landsman to recognize me as soon as he saw me, but he didn't. I sat down at the counter and ordered a strawberry soda with chocolate ice cream. He served me and still there was no sign of recognition.

So I figure, I'm so classy now, how can he identify me with the kid who used to run in for free water? Then when I was in the chips, I'd order a strawberry ice cream soda with chocolate ice cream and tell him to make it "very sweet." Halfway through the soda I'd say "it's too sweet" whereupon he'd fill the glass up again with plain soda. Two sodas for the price of one.

And the note I sustained, with my limp trumpet of a soda straw against the bottom of that empty glass put me right up there with Gabriel and Al Hirt.

I used to read "True Story" in his store for nothing because I wasn't allowed to be reading it at all at home.

Remembering all this I felt a little disappointed that Mr. Landsman still didn't recognize me. Finally, as I paid for my soda, I couldn't stand it anymore so I said, "Mr. Landsman, don't you know who I am?"

"Sure," he said, "Selma."

So I said to him, "I haven't been in this store in nine years. Where do you think I've been?"

So he looks at me and says, "You've been going to the candy store across the street."

I'll never understand why they say, "You can't go home again." I can. They don't even know I've been away.

❧ Everybody Is A
Thomas Wolfe

After Thomas Wolfe published *You Can't Go Home Again,* a lot of people who read it identified with Thomas Wolfe.

Page after page—and there were plenty of pages, it's a thick book—they couldn't get over how Thomas Wolfe was expressing their feelings.

It didn't even matter to them that their emotional experiences were not exactly what Thomas Wolfe was writing about. What got them about the book is that a smart writer like Thomas Wolfe put down on paper *You Can't Go Home Again.*

At least six cases of psychosomatic asthma started breathing normally again. It was such a relief not to go around in constant fear that people would find out about that crumby neighborhood they came from and those crumby people back there.

Thomas Wolfe readers were no longer guilt ridden about those fancy parties they gave on their yachts without inviting the old folks.

Some developed such emotional stability, they stopped sending money home.

Naturally, this did not include Rockefellers or Rothschilds. They could always go home and feel perfectly comfortable because the home they came from was perfectly comfortable.

A famous comedian built a whole routine on how poor he was when he was a kid and that he didn't even know what bread was until he played the Copa.

A famous movie star admitted to an early life of easy virtue because she was so poor she never owned a stitch of clothing until she got her first part in pictures.

Once this sort of thing was taken up by leading citizens of Broadway and Hollywood, it became status to say what had been unsaid.

The daughter of a member of the D.A.R. confided to her date while waiting for the ski lift that she was a direct descendant of an alliance between a bond servant and the scion of a wealthy Seminole family well known in the Everglades.

Her mother had her committed.

Of course, there were some people who had nothing in their backgrounds that couldn't be put on tape and repeated by any talking doll. So they made up stuff about their beginnings.

Blacks, who for generations had produced doctors, lawyers and educators and had never been farther south than N.Y.U., started addressing each other as "boy." Some of them even started contributing money to several civil rights movements which they now referred to as "Our Cause." I don't mind telling you that certain foreign agents reported all this back to their headquarters who became quite alarmed at this upsurge of equality and the leveling of all social classes. They immediately sent back their agents with new orders: OPERATION CAPITALISM.

Every office-seeking liberal who had worked his way through Harvard waiting on tables, became a target.

Copies of a forged Bill of Sale for a Stutz Bearcat mysteriously appeared and turned the voters against him.

An anti-religious group started a rumor that Jesus was not the son of a simple carpenter at all. That, in fact, Joseph was the owner of a very successful unpainted-furniture outlet.

When I read *You Can't Go Home Again* I was still home, so I could read the book quite objectively. There was nothing in the book with which I could identify.

It so happens that at that period of my life I was identifying with "Camille" . . . how I envied her. From the way things were going with me, she was way ahead. It was just my luck that penicillin had been discovered, which blocked my chances for her escape route.

The Armand in my life and I were madly in love. As it neared the end of the school year, there was the constant threat of our being separated. It looked as if he was going to graduate and I wasn't.

In a last desperate effort not to be separated, every day after school, he came over to my house and helped me with my homework. Boy, was his father mad. I'll never forget how Armand and I cried when he told me his father said, "No more running to dumb Selma's house after school. You'll come here to the store and help me with the grocery orders."

Luckily my mother shopped in his father's store, so my Armand would deliver our order first and help me bone up.

From then on until graduation, his and mine, every woman on the block was calling his father on the phone and yelling, "Where's my order? My husband will be home soon and I've got nothing to make for dinner!"

My Furry And Feathered Friends

One day I was in the elevator of the apartment house where I live and a woman walked in with a schnauzer.

Well, when that dog saw me, he smiled. What's more, his tail was going like Sousa was at the other end conducting the Stars and Stripes Forever. You never saw such happiness.

I knew I was a stranger to this dog so I said to the woman at the other end of the leash, "Your dog is mistaking me for somebody he knows."

"Oh no," she says. "He knows you. He hears you on radio and television."

So I said to her, "Your dog hears me on radio?"

And she says, "You see, when we go away, we leave the radio on, so he doesn't get lonesome."

Well, naturally, when I heard this, I bent down and pet the dog. After all, a fan is a fan.

Later I was discussing this incident with a friend of mine and he said that this is not unusual among dog owners and that he also leaves his television set on for his dog when he has to leave him alone.

I got to thinking about this. Before radio and television, when a dog was left alone, I guess he read.

I know, in my home, when we left the dog alone, we used to spread newspapers around. But whoever thought the dog was reading it?

And our dog didn't get any special food. He ate what we ate. Yom Kippur he didn't eat. And I remember during the whole week of Passover he was looped on Manischewitz wine.

When I see the ferris wheels and swings and other toys on sale in pet shops for birds, I can't help feeling it's just a waste of money.

We had two very happy birds and we never thought of buying them anything to play with. We figured, since one bird was a boy and one bird was a girl, they'll think of something. . . .

And we didn't buy them any talking records. You know, the kind that you play for the birds and the birds learn to say what they hear on the record. Our birds learned to say what they heard in the house. One bird used to yell, "Selma, clean up your room" and the other one yelled, "Later."

If I had had to ask for money to buy luxuries for my pets, I wouldn't have had a dog or birds or a chicken of my very own.

Let me explain. . . . It wasn't a chicken when I got it. It was an Easter chick. But by Decoration Day all Easter chicks are chickens.

I'll never forget the friendship that developed between that chicken and our live carp.

The live carp was not intended as a pet. My mother had heard that you can make very good gefilte fish if you get a live carp. So she got one, brought it home, put it into water in the bathtub, assuming that somebody in the family would clobber it.

Well, when we all got some and watched it swimming around so cute in the bathtub, nobody wanted to clobber it.

The whole week that carp was in the bathtub, we were keeping clean by hosing each other down in the cellar.

As I remember, we gave it to our neighbor next door who never became emotionally involved with fish.

❧ Winter Is Banging On The Radiator

Now that we've got all kinds of satellites whizzing through space, there's no limit to the distances with which we can communicate. Which is fine if you want to communicate with great distances. But if you just want to communicate to the janitor in the basement to send up more steam, forget satellites.

The only way to communicate to the janitor to send up more steam is to bang on the radiator.

When I was a small girl, the sounds of winter were my being forcibly fed Scott's Emulsion and my mother's banging on the radiator for more steam.

The purposes for both these activities were never accomplished.

I got just as many colds as the other kids in my class who weren't being forcibly fed Scott's Emulsion and the banging on the radiator didn't bring up more steam.

All the banging ever brought up was the janitor. He'd come walking into our apartment wearing overalls. His arms and chest were always bare. I used to wonder if he wore underwear.

He'd look at us all huddled under sweaters over more sweaters and say, "It's so warm in your apartment. You people must have poor blood."

My mother would point to the bottle of milk on the sill inside the window. The freezing milk would be pushing the bottle top inches above the top of the bottle. Our janitor would look at it and say, "What's that got to do with me? Talk to the crook who's putting water in the milk."

Then, just as the goose bumps would begin to form on his exposed arms from the cold in our apartment, he'd make a dash for the door saying, "If you people didn't have poor blood you wouldn't be cold."

Often he'd run up after my mother's banging on the radiator, look at me bundled up, and say, "It's poor blood, poor blood. My kids are running around downstairs in my apartment in bathing suits."

We all know that to keep their jobs, janitors have to keep proving to the landlord that they're saving him money. In this case, our janitor was also our landlord, so he was especially ambitious to save the landlord money because it was his own money he was saving.

He became a landlord because nobody would rent him an apartment. His problem was a houseful of kids and always more on the way. Christenings were a yearly event with him and his wife and there was some talk in the neighborhood that they seemed to be coming even closer than that.

So Gustave bought this one-family house and to pay for it, it was rented out. He and his family lived in the basement. And it's true that his kids were running around in bathing suits in the basement while we were freezing upstairs. You see, right there with them was the furnace.

But somehow he didn't see it that way. He was convinced that the blazing furnace that kept his family in summer heat all winter sent us springtime at least, and if we didn't feel it, it could only be our poor blood.

When our lease was up we moved. From then on my mother never rented another apartment where there was a janitor-landlord. But no matter where we lived, it seems to me that all my growing-up winters were one bottle of Scott's Emulsion after the other and always banging on the radiator for more steam.

We never got more steam. The winter frost kept pushing the freezing milk up and out of the milk bottle. But we never heard about our poor blood again.

Years later I was walking around at the Food Show in the Coliseum and I bumped into our janitor-landlord and his wife.

All the time we were chatting, I was hoping he'd noticed that, like his wife and himself, I was carrying my coat over my arm. Even after all these years, I wanted him to see that if it was warm, I was warm like everybody else and I didn't have poor blood.

I asked about his children and he told me they were all grown up and it was just his wife and himself living in the basement now. He told me his eldest daughter and her family were living upstairs in the apartment we had.

I said, "I bet you're sending them up plenty of steam."

And he said, "More than plenty. But her husband keeps banging on the radiator. I knew the first time that fellow came to take her out, he looked to me like he had poor blood."

Three

Did You Know Mr. Clean Was Single?

Oh, I must tell you this. A married friend of mine invited me to a party at her place in the country. And she tells me she's sending a bachelor over to drive me up there and mentions that he's a doctor.

So I get dressed and I go downstairs to wait for him and, sure enough, he drives up exactly on time. Just as I get in the car, before we're even out of the driveway, he says, "Let's stop. I want to get the car washed."

So I said, "Get the car washed? What for? We'll be

driving for three-and-a-half hours to get to the country. It'll only get dirty again."

So he says, "I want to have the car washed."

Well, it's his car.

So we stop and I have to get out while he has the car washed.

I get back in the car and I think, what am I doing here with Mr. Clean?

Well, since it's a three-and-a-half-hour drive, I make myself comfortable. I lit a cigarette. Now he's not watching the road, he's watching where I'm putting the ashes.

So I put the cigarette out. I figure, you just meet somebody for the first time, you don't give him trouble. That comes later.

So we drive along. I'm not smoking, but I'm hungry.

So I say, "I'm hungry."

And he says, "Alright, we'll stop at the next restaurant."

So I say, "Oh, let's not get involved with that. Just get some frankfurters and we'll eat those."

At the next roadside stand, we stop and he gets out and comes back with the frankfurters. But he stands outside the car. Now I see he's not going to hand them to me because he doesn't want any eating in his car.

So I get out of the car and eat the frankfurters standing outside.

When I get back in the car I think, who needs this? With this fellow I'll have to give up smoking and eating.

And the more I think about it, the more I get the feeling that I'm with an out patient.

When we get to the party, my friend takes me aside and she says to me, "What do you think of him? He's a very successful doctor."

Well, I'm not going to tell her what I think of him, he's her friend. I can't tell her he's a nut. So I say, "He's very nice."

Then I say, "We didn't talk much. What kind of a doctor is he?"

And she says, "A psychiatrist."

Somehow I got the feeling I should've guessed this.

Anyway, I did not go back with him. I arranged to go back on the caterer's truck with a couple of the hired waiters.

They seemed pretty well-adjusted. You have no idea how much stuff was in that truck that they forgot to serve. It was delicious.

"Understanding" Can Be Hazardous To Your Health

If a fellow calls a girl and breaks a date with her because he has to work late, he expects her to understand. And if she expects him ever to make another date with her, she says, "Of course I understand."

Now, she knows this fellow was ready to pack her in if there was one word out of her about not understanding. But if a girl says, "Of course I understand," a fellow can afford to say, "You're sure you understand?" Then she says, "Don't give it another thought. Of course I understand."

The fellow hangs up radiant with "understanding."

When she hangs up she explodes from "understanding."

To get ready for this date she had spent the whole afternoon in the beauty parlor after promising her boss she would work late the next three nights to catch up.

All three of her roommates are sitting in reserved seats at the Music Hall at her expense since this was not her turn to have the apartment to herself.

What's more, she had been up at five o'clock this morning doing everybody's personal laundry so that it would be out of sight and not in there dripping in case Mr. "Understanding" wanted to use the bathroom.

And now she faces a long, empty frustrating evening.

When her three roommates returned from the Music Hall there are four ready-mix cakes cooling on the kitchen table.

Every casserole in the house, a chafing dish and two milk bottles are filled with D-Zerta.

Stitches had been cast on for a jumbo knit sweater and everybody's laundry had been done over and is dripping in the bathroom.

She's in bed asleep. Her fresh hairdo is wrapped in shocking pink boutique toilet tissue. On the night table next to her is an untouched glass of non-fat milk and an unopened carton of diet cookies.

There is also an empty beer can, an empty ginger ale bottle, a spoon standing upright in a half-eaten jar of peanut butter, a crescent of crust left over from a moon of pizza "with everything on it" and two frozen egg rolls slowly defrosting.

Boy, was I sick the next day.

On the other hand, when I'm working late and have to break a date, I never say I'm working late because there isn't a man in the world who ever takes a girl's job seriously.

So what I usually say is that I can't make the date because I'm ill in bed.

A man always understands this because after all "I'm only a girl."

And I've discovered that it helps to be specific about the illness. So whatever is seasonal, for that time of the year, that's what I've got.

In the winter it's a terrible cold, in the summer poison ivy, spring and fall it's whatever is catching.

Since TV writing involves a lot of last minute changes, writing and rewriting and very often long into the night, I have to break dates quite often.

As a matter of fact, there are some fellows dating me who don't even know exactly what I do for a living. All they know is that my health is very delicate.

I get an awful lot of bed jackets for Christmas.

How Blind Is A Blind Date?

One evening I was having dinner with a fellow and the conversation got around to blind dates. He told me that before he even goes out on a blind date he knows pretty much how it's going to turn out. What's more, he knows what blind dates to avoid entirely.

He said he avoids all blind dates that his friends try to make for him with their girl cousins.

"Once the whole family is pitching in to get a cousin dates," he explained, "you can be sure they're desperate to unload what is fast becoming a discontinued number, so they can display what's in style now."

"If she happens to be a girl cousin from out of town," he continued, "I know they're bringing her in because she's already bombed in her hometown and the family is hoping word of it hasn't gotten out."

Then he told me about blind dates he would like to avoid but can't because of social or business obligations . . . especially sisters of brothers he is friendly with or with whom he does business.

"When you're out with a friend's sister," he explained, "you might just as well be out with a friend's brother. There's no fun in asking her up to your apartment because while you're asking her, you're asking yourself 'Would you want this to happen to *your* sister?'

"Even if she suddenly wants to see if your apartment is anything like her brother's, it's no sign that things may pick up. All it means is that she wants to see if your apartment is anything like her brother's."

It looked to me as if his face began to sadden now.

"Divorcées," he said, "regardless of the word around town, are a pretty disenchanting group. Especially if they have been divorcées for any length of time. You can't suddenly float a mothball fleet."

"What about the numbers in that 'little black book' passed on to you by a friend when he gets married?" I asked him.

"I already have those numbers," he said. "Everybody's 'little black book' is just a duplicate of the same numbers."

I didn't know that. I wonder if the Xerox company knows that their product has speeded up efficiently not only during office hours but after office hours as well.

My dinner date interrupted his discussion of blind dates to call for the check. I went to the Ladies' Room to think.

I started to think. I'm not this fellow's friend's cousin from out of town. I'm not the sister of a friend of his. I'm not a divorcée and my number isn't in everybody's "little black book."

I powdered my nose and joined him. As we left the restaurant I was sure I'd soon find out what kind of blind date he had me figured for.

I Only Wear Glasses To See

When *Look* called and asked me if they could do a picture story on me out on a date, I agreed. That's no problem.

Then they called again and asked me to provide my date. I agreed. Now that was a problem.

If I asked somebody I liked to appear in the picture story with me, he might think I'm moving in for the kill and I'd never see him again.

If I asked somebody I didn't like, who needs his picture?

Rather than disturb the status quo of my current social relationships I decided to invite a fellow with whom I share a mutual uninvolved, unemotional indifference.

Some women call this kind of relationship "being friends with a man." I call it what it is—"nothing."

Men are friends with men. Women are friends with women. When a man and woman are friends, it means nothing to him that she's a woman and it means nothing to her that he's a man.

For example: If you're "just friends" he thinks there's nothing wrong in calling you up at a quarter to eight in the evening and saying, "I'm stuck with a couple of theater tickets and you're the only girl I would dare call on such short notice."

Or you might get a call, "I was just on my way to the driving range to shoot a pail of golf balls but it's raining too hard. So if it doesn't stop in half an hour I'll call you back and take you to dinner."

See what I mean? "Nothing."

I called the first man on my "nothing" list. His name begins with "A."

I have quite a few of these relationships so I list them alphabetically.

I said, "Hello 'A,' this is 'S.'"

I'm sure he has a list too.

I said, "How would you like to take me to dinner?"

"I just took you to dinner," he said.

"That was three weeks ago," I said.

"That's right," he said. "I just took you to dinner three weeks ago." Then he said, "I've gotta rush. I'm on my way to the driving range to shoot a pail of balls."

"Wait a minute," I said.

And I told him about *Look* and the story they were planning on me.

"In that case," he said, "I'll be glad to help. That's what friends are for."

Even if this fellow's name didn't begin with "A," I would still put him at the top of my "nothing" list.

I picked him up in my cab the night the pictures were to be taken and we drove to the restaurant the magazine had chosen as a background.

We were to be photographed as we had dinner together.

As the waiter handed me the menu and the photographer started taking our pictures, I said to my friend, "Please read the menu to me so I can tell you what I'd like to eat."

In front of the waiter and the photographer he says, "Why do you always come out without your glasses? You know you can't see without them."

That's a man for a friend. I'd rather he was a diplomatic enemy.

I said, "I don't have to wear my glasses all the time. My eyesight isn't that bad."

Now he starts laughing and he says to me, "That's really funny. I guess you forgot what happened the last time you came out without your glasses."

I'll tell you what happened the last time. There are two movie houses in my neighborhood which are really one building. They share the same entrance but play different features. In the movie house to the left the Ladies' Room is to the left of the lobby. In the movie house next to it everything is reversed.

Well, the last time it was raining too hard for my friend to shoot a pail of golf balls, he took me to the movies. I didn't have my glasses with me that evening either. When we went into the lobby I didn't stop to think about reversed positions and walked into the Men's Room.

He never stopped me.

❧ President Johnson Helped Love Find A Way

There was a lot to cheer about with the passage of the Civil Rights legislation during the Johnson Administration and we're all still cheering.

But, there was another progressive step that was taken under the Johnson Administration for which President Johnson was solely responsible.

There should have been some cheering about this, too.

Do you realize that when President Johnson gave his blessing to Luci Baines' marriage even though Luci was younger than Lynda Bird, he pointed the road to a new freedom.

That's right, a new freedom.

For generations, on the continent and with continental nationals in this country, it was strictly forbidden for a younger daughter to marry while the elder daughter was unmarried.

There could be no compromise. Seniority took priority over love, romance and whatever bridaled or unbridaled passions pursued the younger.

This custom was inviolate for fear that if the younger got married before the elder, the elder would be passed over forever, and forever remain unmarried.

Well, Lyndon just said "poof" to all that and his younger daughter Luci got married. And what do you know, Lynda didn't get passed over at all. Within the year she got married too.

Now, aren't the ways of the New World better than those of the Old World?

Do you know the kind of things that used to happen before President Johnson led the way to a new order?

My grandmother told me what happened to two sisters, not unlike Luci and Lynda, and their father, who was definitely unlike Lyndon.

Love, romance and proposals of marriage constantly appeared for the younger sister. But the father withheld his permission for her to marry because the older sister just wasn't moving off the shelf.

Unfortunately, the younger sister's suitors would all get tired of waiting and would soon be on their way. And though others followed, they too would soon become discouraged.

While the older sister was quite happy unmarried, the younger was not. So when their father's business

took them to another town, the younger sister suggested that since they were unknown in this new town,
she would pass for being the older. All this poor kid
wanted was a break and the father, being a father,
agreed.

So what happens now that the younger sister is the
older sister and the older is the younger to their new
neighbors? The younger sister, who is really the older
sister, finds love, romance and a suitor in the new town
where she is known as the younger sister.

But her father withheld his permission for her to
marry. What would the people in their new town say if
the younger sister got married before the older sister?

✐ Who Made "30" The Closing Date?

I don't go to class reunions anymore.
I used to go the first couple of years after I got out of
school. But as the years and years and years passed, I
gave it up. Men keep on going to class reunions. Women
drop out and for a very good reason. What woman is

going to walk into a room where every other woman there knows exactly how old she is?

You know what the whole problem is? In this country we worship youth. If you're not young you're supposed to think young. I suppose that's okay, but what good is it? All the time I'm thinking young I'm getting older.

What's more, we're all lying about our ages. And to make the lie stick, when somebody comes up with a topic about the past, you say "I don't remember . . ." hoping all the time that the idea is getting across that you were too young to remember.

I do it too. I've spent evenings with people where there were so many things brought up that "I don't remember" that when I leave I wonder . . . Did I give the impression that I'm young or that I'm an amnesia victim?

What's so nutty about it is that no matter what age you are, you do it.

I have a friend whose mother must be in her sixties, but is very chic. The minute something loosens up, she runs and has it tightened.

Well, my friend was telling me about the time she took her young son to visit his grandmother.

While he was over there, he found a picture book which was a collection of old-time movie stars.

Naturally all the faces of those old-time movie stars were totally unfamiliar to him. He took the book over to his grandmother and pointing to one of the pictures he said, "Grandma, who was Rudolph Valentino?" And this sixty-year-old lady said to him, "Ask your mother, I don't remember silent pictures."

I once went up to the country to one of those places that cater to young unmarrieds. After I checked in, I figured I'd go around the pool.

It's around the pool where you find the action.

And sure enough, a fellow comes over and invites me into the pool with him, to swim, that is. I said to him, "I can't swim." It so happens that I can swim but I know that to get the action going immediately you must have a weakness.

"I'll teach you," he said.

I let him. I had noticed him before he had come over to talk to me. If he had invited me to take a walk, I would have let him teach me how to do that. He was kind of cute and I figured we could make it.

After my swimming lesson, in which I displayed an unusually inept talent, he set up a physical-fitness program for me, personally supervised by him.

He was going to instruct me in swimming, rowing, drinking before dinner, drinking after dinner, tennis, golf and whatever other facilities were provided for by this resort hotel.

Well, I'm thinking, I just checked in and already I've got it made.

As I cling helplessly to him, barely managing to keep my balance walking up a very smooth lawn, he hits me with it. "I'm so glad you showed up," he says. "I was getting so tired of the 'young ones.'"

This was the end for me, because at that time I was twenty-four for the *first* time . . .

And lately it seems to me that everything in the stores is to attract the young.

Especially in the fall. Everything is "back to college." No matter what store you walk into it's all "back to college."

As far as the stores are concerned, if you happen to be a high school drop-out, you can run around naked.

What's more, the stores are staffed with college girls who are there to advise you on the right thing to wear for every occasion.

This does nothing for me. I doubt very much if I'll be going to any fraternity dances.

Now on the Continent a woman ages like wine. In our country the minute you stop fizzing they start opening another bottle.

Over there, if you're a woman, you're a sex symbol.

In Paris, even during the day, you see couples of all ages walking along the street kissing and holding hands.

I like to see that. I once stopped to ask directions in Paris. The *gendarme* took my hand, looked into my eyes and directed me to Napoleon's Tomb as if we were spending the weekend together.

I always think of Paris as a great big motel.

Four

The Marquis Of Queensberry Was A Marriage Counselor

I always think of marriage as an honest relationship between two people who like each other.

When I say honest relationship I mean a friendly one.

Not the kind of honest relationship where she says to him, "If you want my honest opinion, you're getting bald."

Or he says to her, "If you want my honest opinion, you're getting bald."

I'm talking about an honest, friendly relationship.

Like if you get up in the middle of the night and you're thirsty, you can poke your partner and say, "I'm thirsty."

And he says, "You're thirsty, then get up and get yourself a drink of water."

See, he honestly does not want to get out of bed to get her a drink of water—and quite honestly she didn't expect him to. That's friendly.

But according to a new theory for happy marriages that some psychologist has just come up with, I'm all wrong.

This psychologist says couples who don't fight aren't happily married.

When she pokes him to tell him she's thirsty, she's got to poke hard enough to draw blood.

He doesn't even say a word, just lets her have it on the side of the head.

The idea is that if you're getting married don't look for a partner. What you want is an opponent.

Any marriage that starts off with "I love you" hasn't got a chance.

The three little words on your Valentine are "Put 'em up!"

Can you imagine going down to the New York State Boxing Commission for a marriage license?

As for the wedding itself, no more walking down the aisle. The bridal couple will just square off as the preacher says, "I now pronounce you man and wife. Break clean and come out fighting."

I hate to think that what every bride should know is how to protect yourself in the clinches.

🎐 May I Have The Envelope Please?

You know how they always give an annual award for the best acting in movies, TV and the theater.

Well, they're leaving out a very important category of acting which is as much deserving of an award and recognition as anything else around.

I think there should be an award given in recognition of the acting a girl has to give at her surprise bridal shower.

Every girl knows that when her wedding date is set, her friends are going to give her a surprise bridal shower. Because when a girl's wedding date is set, her friends always give her a surprise wedding shower.

This is the one premarital activity for which her friends are responsible.

Any other premarital activity in which the bride-to-be engages is her own responsibility.

There isn't a playwright alive or dead who has ever written a more challenging acting role than that of the bride-to-be at her surprise bridal shower.

When she opens the door and her friends yell "Surprise!" this girl acts so surprised she could give Helen Hayes lessons.

She almost faints. She cries. She hugs everybody. She calls everybody by name.

Now you've got to admit this is pretty good acting for a kid who while she's giving out with all this is also counting the house, the number of gifts piled on the table and already has it figured that two of the girls are freeloaders.

Another important thing to remember is that this is the first time she's played to an audience of more than one.

Up until now, her innocent Ophelia was only for the groom-to-be on their first date.

Again he was her only audience, when as sweet Juliet, she surrendered to him during Single's Weekend at Grossinger's.

He stopped to say "hello" to a girl in the lobby when they were checking out. Driving home in the car, she did such a convincing Medea that when Judith Anderson heard about it, she ran out and bought a candy store.

It takes real talent unwrapping gift wrappings and carefully putting aside each ribbon rosette, folding the gift wrappings, carefully lifting out one sheet of tissue paper after the other and all the time acting as if a ribbon rosette, gift wrapping and sheets of tissue paper are enough of a gift for her.

And how about the way she sustains the high pitch of her excitement after unwrapping six identical gift ice-buckets?

It takes rare talent to keep breaking up, reading that funny stuff her friends wrote on the enclosed cards.

I think this field of acting should be recognized. I'm surprised Cosmopolitan isn't doing it.

I also think the winner's coach should be recognized —her mother. You saw how surprised she was and she planned the shower with the girls.

Finish Your Cereal Or No Wedding

A young girl student from one of the nearby women's colleges came around to interview me for her school paper.

Right away she started asking me questions. She

wanted to know did I think a writing career takes the place of marriage.

Well, that's ridiculous. Everybody knows you can't warm your feet on the back of a typewriter.

Then she wanted my opinion on premarital relationships, extramarital relationships and how old a woman should be before she has any kind of sex relationships.

So I said to her, "Hold it, kid. Is this all you girls up at your school want to read about?"

"Not me," she says. "I've been married since my senior year in high school."

Now I started asking her questions. "How long have you been married?"

"Four years," she said.

"What did your parents say about your getting married this young?" I asked.

"My husband and I kept it a secret until the babies started coming."

Naturally that would be a dead giveaway.

"How many babies do you have?" I asked her.

"Only three," she said.

"You've been married four years and you only have three babies. What's been holding you up?"

"Last year I flunked math and I had to go to summer school to catch up."

The way this kid has been putting two and two together I'll never understand how she flunked math.

I was curious about her husband so I said, "What does your husband do?"

"He teaches school," she told me. "That's how I met him. I was in his class."

She'll catch up. Look who she's got helping her with her homework.

It seems to me that every time I go to a wedding, the bridal couple seems to be getting younger and younger. At the last one I didn't know who was the ring bearer and who was the groom. For a moment there the rabbi didn't either. The ring bearer wouldn't give up the ring. The only way they finally got it away from him was to let him slip it on the bride's finger.

A friend of mine told me he went to a wedding recently where the bride cried all night because the groom got a bigger piece of wedding cake than she did.

It's an awful chore buying wedding presents for these kids. Where are you going to find a "His and Hers" pencil box? You have to buy two of everything or they fight over it.

I wonder if F. A. O. Schwarz has Brides' Registry.

Some Husbands Are As Smart As Their Wives

It's not unusual for a wife to go shopping, tell her husband the dress she bought cost twice as much as it really did and then pocket the difference.

Her argument is "you never know." That "you never know" may sometimes mean "you never know when we'll need it."

But the only time it's been "you never know when we'll need it" was the one time I saw a movie in which a nice actress like maybe Jeanne Crain, playing a wife, gave her little bundle back to her husband when the barn burned down. That was a movie. What happens in movies doesn't happen in real life.

I bet if Jeanne Crain is married in real life she also . . . no, why should I talk about her, I don't even know her. I wouldn't be a bit surprised if she . . . and if she does, it's none of my business.

I'll just talk about my friends. I have friends who do that.

I also have a friend who works it the other way.

When she buys a dress she tells him it only cost half as much.

She has to work it this way because her mother is loaded and has generously offered her daughter and son-in-law sums of money. The son-in-law happens to be one of these nuts who won't take money from anybody unless he's earned it.

So mother and daughter have worked out a system that keeps the husband happy. They don't tell him what's going on.

What's going on is that when the daughter goes shopping with her mother and sees two dresses she likes, she pays for one dress with her husband's money and her mother buys her the second dress. This also goes on with shoes, hats, blouses, and even handbags.

Well, to explain to her husband how come she always buys two dresses, two pair of shoes and two of whatever else she buys, she just cuts the actual prices in half.

This had been going on since she'd been married and she thought she was getting away with it.

She became pregnant and as her time of lying in drew close her doctor asked her to bring in her husband on her next visit, as he wanted to talk to both of them.

On her next visit to the doctor she arrived with her husband and the doctor announced that he was sure now that instead of one baby, the wife was going to have twins.

Like a shot, the husband turned to his wife and said, "Boy, I've got to hand it to your mother."

The Mother-In-Law Who Isn't A Joke

A couple of years ago out on the coast, I was working with another comedy writer who had just married a very talented and attractive television actress.

At the end of the TV season I came East to work on another show and didn't see this writer again for about two years.

He came East on a visit and called me to have dinner with him.

While we were having dinner I asked him how his wife was and he tells me they're divorced.

"I'm sorry," I said.

"It's a pretty unpleasant business," he said. "Somehow I expected it to be a little easier the second time."

This rather startled me, so I said, "You mean you've been married twice and divorced twice in just the past two years. That's really moving. You must've started going with your second wife while you were on your honeymoon with your first wife."

"You could say that," he says, "because it's my first wife I divorced, married again and divorced again."

Then he tells me what happened. The first time they got married it didn't work at all. Her career kept her so busy she didn't have time to be a wife and make a home for him. The second time it was great.

When he got home from work his dinner was always waiting for him. The house was immaculate. His socks were always darned and he was happier than an airline stewardess with an all-male passenger list.

He sighed, "I sure miss all that now."

So I said, "No wonder you miss your wife."

"Who's talking about my wife," he said. "She didn't do anything to make our marriage work the second time any more than she did the first time. It's my mother-in-law I miss. She came to live with us the second time we got married and ran the house. My wife busted us up."

"Are you telling me you fell in love with your mother-in-law?"

"Don't be silly," he said. "She's old enough to be my mother-in-law. But I can't begin to tell you how happy I was with her around."

"That's a switch," I said.

"I'm never going to write another mother-in-law joke again as long as I live," he continued. "It's wife jokes I'm writing from now on. Wives are the troublemakers. Everything was going along great until my wife brought a television director home for dinner and that was the beginning of the end of my remarriage."

"I get it now," I said. "Your wife left you for this director."

"No such luck," he said. "This director went for my mother-in-law. He started romancing her and they got married. That was the end of my happy home. If my wife hadn't brought that director around, my mother-in-law would still be living with us.

"Believe me," he said, "wives with their interfering break up more homes than mothers-in-law."

The Unfulfilled Housewife And What Unfulfilled Her

You hear an awful lot these days about the unfulfilled housewife . . . especially from the unfulfilled housewife.

She's sitting around in her pottery class, keeping her clay damp with her own tears as she and her sisterhood, awaiting their turn at the kiln, talk about what has brought them to this fiery furnace.

They agree that it's the frustration of not being needed anymore in their natural role of loving wife, mother and homemaker.

They blame their loss of identity on Uncle Ben's Instant Rice. What's more shattering than rice which is not only cooked in an instant but is so perfect every time that on the plate each grain salutes you?

This, of course, from those whose rice involvement used to be spread over forty minutes of watchful simmering in a hot kitchen. Forty minutes of life they gave to their rice, at the end of which time, not only wasn't there any saluting . . . you were lucky if that rice stood at attention.

The identity crisis in which the loving mother now finds herself because her twenty-two-year-old son does not need her to dress him anymore is also on the wrong track.

As for the loving wife, whose career-ridden husband comes home too tired for sex, she really has no problem. In this permissive society, what's good enough for your daughter is good enough for you.

So what is it that is causing the ever-rising demand for modeling clay? What is it that has so broken American womanhood that even as she stands in front of her fellow Weight Watchers as the member with the largest weight loss of the week, she doesn't feel like a winner?

What joy is there in taking a fat friend shopping with you while you slip in and out of every size ten and some large size eights when you're nothing.

And what is the real torment of the American housewife? It's having the painters in. This is where you are destroyed as an identity.

What woman feels like anything when she goes through what she has to go through when the painters are coming. I don't have to tell you what you have to go through. And you have to go through all this yourself.

First of all, since your husband comes home too tired for sex he's too tired to help you take everything out of the closets.

Your daughter isn't around to help you because she's busy getting ready for the painters in the apartment she shares with three airline hostesses who can't help her because this is their transatlantic flight week.

And you can't ask your twenty-two-year-old son who doesn't need you to dress him anymore. For three weeks now he's been protesting with a "sit-in" in his room because you wouldn't let him make an underground movie.

Now how are you going to get him out of his room so the painters can get in without asking your Canasta group to let him film all of you playing without any clothes on? It's these pressures mounting up because the painters are coming which are driving women up the wall.

And after the painters leave, where are you?

All over the world women are asking themselves this same question.

When Nora ran out of her Doll's House in the middle of the night screaming, "I've got to get out of here," what do you think really drove her out? It wasn't her husband. It wasn't her kid. It wasn't her doll-like existence. It was the smell of paint.

Nora had just had her place done. It's cold in Norway. Open a window to let the smell out and you freeze. Keep the windows closed and you can die from the smell.

Show me a woman who looks forward to having the painters in and I'll show you a real nut.

Craig's wife is a classic example of this. She couldn't even wait three years between paint jobs, she enjoyed it so much. So her husband ran out in the middle of the night screaming, "I've got to get out of here."

I visited Nora and Craig in their love nest. And rather than go through again what I went through with the painters the last time, I wired them to find out if there was an igloo for rent in their neighborhood. Because I've got to get out of here.

I don't remember if it was because of the painters' strike or the Mets on a winning streak, but by the time the painters went back to work, all the boss could send me was one man.

Even though I have a small apartment, one man working alone is endless.

That painter spent more time in my apartment than

Michelangelo spent in the Sistine Chapel. What's more, I doubt if my ceiling is going to last as long. It certainly doesn't look as good, either.

He was around for days and days. I never thought when I hired that painter, I was getting a roommate.

Painters, as you know, show up at eight o'clock in the morning. Well, at that hour in the morning I'm just getting out of bed. So when I'd open the door to let him in, he'd always see me in my bathrobe. Under these circumstances how formal can you be? After the first week, we were on a first-name basis.

I must say I wasn't too happy with this relationship. What's the big thrill being shacked up with a fellow whose idea of shaving lotion is turpentine?

Also, I was stuck with a color-blind painter.

The first time I came home from work I looked at the living-room walls and said, "That's not the color I picked out."

So he says, "That's your color but it dries darker."

I walked into the bedroom and looked at the walls and said, "What's that!"

So he says, "That color dries lighter."

No matter what color you pick out for the bathroom, that never dries.

All the time that painter was in my apartment, I couldn't use the bathroom. And this was no crummy painter. He came very highly recommended. As a matter of fact, I was told he was Jacqueline Onassis's painter.

So I was thinking that she must've gone through

what I'm going through. All the time the painter was there, Jacqueline Onassis couldn't use the bathroom. And she's got kids. With kids you need a bathroom. I guess she did what I did.

Can you imagine a rich lady like Jacqueline Onassis running around in the hall to see if there's a neighbor who'll let her use the bathroom?

Five

Sometimes Blood
Is Thinner
Than Water

To my aunt the whole world is Jewish. No matter what famous man's birthday comes up for celebration, as far as she's concerned, he was Jewish.

Every year on Washington's Birthday she says, "Did you know George Washington was Jewish?"

Lincoln's Birthday; Lincoln was Jewish. The man who shot Lincoln wasn't, but Lincoln was.

On Columbus Day she reminds you that Columbus

was Jewish. And you can't argue her out of this. Of course with Christmas there's no argument.

Living in the Space Age, she too has broadened her horizons. Watching Neil Armstrong on television take "one giant step for mankind" she turned to her son-in-law and said, "In America, who knows if Armstrong is his real name."

Secure in the thought that the whole world is united, my dear aunt uses all her energies to unite her immediate family. She's the one who organized our family circle. In this way, she dreamed, the family would meet as a unit to share mutual interests and mutual benefits.

At these meetings the poor relatives always show up early and the rich relatives show up late. Who's in a hurry when they know that before the meeting's over they'll be co-signing a note?

My aunt has never successfully housebroken her pet dog because, rather than use violence or even the threat of violence, she has insisted on reasoning with a three-week-old schnauzer.

Yet should any member of the family try to get out of attending the next meeting of the family circle she is ready to unleash destructive forces against you and yours for generations to come. As she puts it to all of us, "Don't forget, I've got your number."

And she has. When Uncle Bernard challenged her with, "What do you mean you've got my number?" she said, "You think I don't know about you and the ladies' handbag buyer from Cleveland."

Cousin Zimmie's number is the address where her daughter, away at college, gets her mail and the other address where she's living.

I once tried to get out of going to a meeting and she hit me with, "Would you like me to call up Jack O'Brien and tell him exactly how old you are?"

While the thought of this is agonizing enough, she holds even a bigger threat over my head. If I antagonize my aunt, she'll cut off my supply of chicken fat.

The meeting I tried unsuccessfully to avoid was what my aunt called an emergency meeting.

Let me explain about my aunt's emergencies.

I have a cousin who's a doctor and my aunt called an emergency meeting. You know what the emergency was? He started going with a poor girl.

According to my aunt, wasn't it enough his father paid to make him a doctor? If he is going with a poor girl, that means her father can't pay to open an office for him. And after making him a doctor where was the money going to come from for the office?

Another emergency we once met to meet was that my cousin Ethel's daughter-in-law didn't call Ethel "mother." She called Ethel "Ethel" or "you" and referred to her as "she."

We also had an emergency meeting when cousin Samson's daughter Gloria eloped.

This was a very short meeting. A resolution was passed unanimously: No wedding! No presents!

So when my aunt called me about this new emergency, I was just being polite when I asked, "What's the emergency?"

"Remember," she says, "you've heard us talk about this burial plot we bought many years ago way out in the country. Well, we've had it all these years and there's nobody in it."

So I said, "What's the meeting? A call for volunteers?"

At the meeting Uncle Bernard gets up and starts explaining that this property is in an area that has been rezoned so that the adjoining community wants to buy it to build a shopping center.

I jumped right up and said, "Let's sell it." Because, to tell you the truth, I'd rather go shopping than that other thing.

So my uncle says to me, "College girl—"

When my uncle says "college girl" he is reminding the family again that without any education, starting as a glazier he has become one of the biggest builders in the city and can buy and sell all of us.

Incidentally, outside of this one irritating habit, he's really a very nice guy. If any member of the family moves into one of his buildings, he puts in a glass shower door free.

Anyway, as he was saying to me, "College girl, don't you understand? If we sell this land, you not only won't be able to go shopping, when your time comes, you won't have any place to lie down."

So I said, "Don't worry about it. Let's sell the property. I'm sure when my time comes, friends will bury me."

So he says, "Whoever heard of such a thing? Relatives bury you."

Then he says, "We're together on this earth. We should all be together in the afterworld."

Right here, my aunt applauded.

I just didn't have the heart to tell them that I'm not too happy with all of them in this world.

Instead I said, "I'll tell you what. Let's sell the property and I promise you that in the afterworld I'll look you up."

Which of course I have no intention of doing. What's more, it won't be easy for them to look me up either because when I get to heaven I'm getting an unlisted harp.

Save The Saks' Box

One year, just before the Fourth of July, my aunt called me and said, "You heard?"

I said, "What?"

She said, "You didn't hear?"

I said, "What?"

So she said, "A terrible thing happened in Philadelphia."

I said, "What?"

So she said, "The worst thing that could happen, happened in Philadelphia."

So I said, "The British are back."

"Worse," she said. "The professor called me. The wedding is off."

Let me explain about the term "professor" as my aunt uses it. To my aunt, anybody in the family who teaches school is a professor. And I have a lot of cousins who teach school. As a matter of fact until I started to go to school, I thought "professor" was the Yiddish word for "cousin."

My aunt continued, "Think of it, the professor's daughter is a marriage drop-out."

"Look," I said, "this sort of thing happens. It's not that terrible."

"It's worse than terrible," she said. "You didn't know the professor took off his own Masonic ring and gave it to his daughter's 'to-be.' He even had it made smaller, at his own expense, to fit his future son-in-law-that's-not-to-be's little finger. Now it's going to cost him to make his Masonic ring big again to fit his little finger."

"I guess the couple found out that they weren't right for each other and decided not to go through with the wedding," I said.

"Who finds out such a thing before the wedding,"

she said. "You find out after the wedding that you can't get along."

"I don't understand why you're getting so upset," I said. "It's not your problem so just ignore it."

"How can I ignore it," she said, "when I think of that poor unhappy single girl?"

"Don't worry about her," I said. "A girl can be single, make a life for herself and be happy and fulfilled."

"Selma," she said, "wash your mouth out with soap."

Then she said to me, "Don't you realize what a terrible thing this is? The money that was already spent. They put down a deposit on the caterer. They sent out invitations. People had shoes dyed.

"And what about the wedding presents?"

"What about the wedding presents?" I asked. "That's no problem. You just send them back to the people who sent them and they'll take them back to the store."

"What're you talking about, 'they'll take them back to the store'?" she said.

"That's it," I said. "And they'll get their money back."

"How can they do that?" she said. "Everybody bought wholesale."

"Well," I said, "she can send mine back to me, because I didn't buy wholesale."

So my aunt said, "How is she going to know which is your present?"

"That's simple," I said, "I went into Saks, bought a present and the present is in a Saks' box."

"Answer me," she said. "How is she going to know which is your present?"

"It's in a Saks' box," I said.

So she now says, "But everybody who buys wholesale puts it in a Saks' box!"

❧ Nepotism Or How I Got My Ears Pierced

My aunt never starts a phone conversation with me by saying "hello." And when she finishes talking, she just hangs up. She never says "goodbye" to me, either.

I've been around when she's had phone conversations with other people and I've noticed she says "hello" and "goodbye" to them.

So one day I asked her, "How come you say 'hello' and 'goodbye' when you're talking on the phone to everybody but me?"

So she says, "I'm your aunt. Those formalities are for strangers."

Another thing that happens when she calls me on the

phone is that I get the feeling she's started her conversation with me sometime between deciding to call me and the time I answered the phone.

I've picked up my phone to hear her say, ". . . so that's why I called you."

Once, the first thing I heard from her was, ". . . everything to live for. The funeral is tomorrow."

One day I answered the phone and she was saying, ". . . the letter for the physical."

So I said, "What physical?"

She says, "Didn't you get the letter to go for a physical?"

While she's talking, I'm thinking, a letter to go for a physical? I must be drafted. But that's impossible unless some joker is fixing up a blind date between me and Moshe Dayan.

"Start from the beginning," I asked.

She started where she usually starts, somewhere in the middle. ". . . and that's why I made an appointment for you to go to Cousin Helen's boy for a check-up. The boy who just became a doctor. He needs patients."

"Thank you very much," I said, "but I just had a check-up and my doctor says everything is okay."

"Are you sure he checked everything?" she said.

"Of course I'm sure," I said. "Because when I went to the doctor, I had everything with me."

"Then you should definitely go," she says. "A healthy person can give a new doctor a lot of confidence. Take a pencil and write down his office address."

Well, she gives me the address and it's in Philadelphia.

So I said, "Philadelphia! Who needs a doctor in Philadelphia? I'm in New York."

"Keep the address handy," she says to me. "You could get sick in the middle of the night and you'll need a doctor in a hurry."

I said, "So I'm going to call a doctor in Philadelphia?"

"Keep the address," she says. "Where in New York will you get a doctor to make a house call in the middle of the night?"

You know, I wrote down the address. But I told her to cancel the appointment she made for my check-up.

I shy away from beginners. When my cousin Arthur was beginning as a dentist, my aunt made an appointment for me with him.

I went. This young dentist was so nervous just examining my teeth that he kept dropping all his instruments. And they were dropping in my mouth.

He kept yelling, "Don't swallow, don't swallow!"

He wasn't worried about me. Those instruments weren't all paid for.

By the time he finished examining my teeth I needed four stitches.

I said to him, "Take it easy."

"It's not my fault," he says. "You're jumping up and down in the chair."

Sure I was jumping up and down in the chair. Instead of brushing, this kid was drilling.

When I left there, he hadn't hit my teeth once . . . but he pierced my ears.

Another thing my aunt does besides rounding up patients for novice professionals to practice on is round up paying customers for those in business enterprises.

If anybody in the family opens a store, she calls up and says, "It wouldn't hurt you to give them a little business."

Well, that's no problem. Somebody in the family opened a children's clothing store, so whenever I have to buy a gift for a child, I buy it there.

I have another relative who owns a lamp store. That's no problem either. A lamp makes a nice housewarming present.

The only relative who is a problem owns a surgical appliance store. I have no friends who ever lift anything heavy.

❧ *Mink Is A*
Four-Letter Word

My aunt's measure of respectability, connubial bliss and financial stability is a black Persian lamb coat.

You see, not everybody can afford it. It's warm and it wears well.

According to her, a man who buys one for his wife is obviously a good provider and is warmly appreciative of how well the woman he married is wearing.

Mink, however, is a measure of something else again.

A man who buys his wife a mink coat is hiding something. A girl wearing a mink coat is what he is hiding.

So when I showed up wearing a mink coat she said to me, "I see you're wearing a new muskrat coat."

I said, "It's mink."

"To tell the truth," she said, "on somebody else I would think it's mink. On you I know it's muskrat."

I said, "It's mink."

Now she gives me a co-conspirator's smile and says, "You think I don't know what's going on nowadays. A lady in my Canasta group who's married to a furrier told me how they dye and let-out muskrat to look like mink."

"This is mink, " I said.

"Mink mink?" she asked.

"Mink mink," I said.

"You won it in a raffle," she hoped.

"No," I said.

"You know somebody in the fur business who gave you a bargain," she hoped some more.

"No," I said.

One thing about my aunt. With her, hope really springs eternal.

"You borrowed it from a girl friend," she sprung.

"No," I said, "I went into a store and bought it."

"Retail?" she said.

"That's right," I said.

"Are you trying to tell me," she said, "that a single girl walks into a retail store and buys a mink coat?"

And I said, "Yes, I did that."

And as I spoke, it hit me, as it must've hit her at the same time, that buying your own mink coat is like mass rejection. A fact as bitter to my aunt as shacking up with a married man.

Just then there was a knock on her door, and she said to me, "It's my neighbor! Hide the coat!"

℘ Everybody Is In Show Biz

When Stanley Kramer was making a movie called "It's A Mad, Mad, Mad, Mad World" he asked me to be the voice of Spencer Tracy's wife.

Well, I don't have to tell you how excited I got about this because Spencer Tracy had always been my Richard Burton. Unfortunately, I had never been his Elizabeth Taylor.

Of course, I wanted to go out to Hollywood to do the picture and I was telling my aunt about it.

So I said to her, "Can you imagine me going out to Hollywood to do a picture directed by Stanley Kramer?"

So she says to me, "Why not?"

So I said to her, "What do you mean, 'why not?' I've never made a movie before."

So she says to me, "Do they have to know?"

When I went out in stock for John Kenley to do "Bye Bye Birdie" with Andy Williams I told her about that too and she said to me, "What kind of part will you be playing?"

"I play Andy Williams' mother," I said.

"His real mother," she said, "or his father's second wife?"

"His real mother," I said. "There's no father in the play. I'm a widow."

"I don't like it," she said.

I said, "What do you mean you don't like it?"

"I don't like it," she said.

So I said to her, "What're you making such a big thing out of this? I like acting and this is a chance for me."

So she says to me, "What chance does a widow have with a grown son!"

She's also very critical of my TV appearances. Once she called me after the Tonight Show and she said to me, "You're doing a terrible thing on TV."

So I said to her, "Please, I'm doing the best I can."

So she says to me, "I want to help you."

So I said, "Okay. What's the terrible thing I'm doing on TV?"

"You're looking fat," she says.

"Looking fat," I said. "I can't do anything about that. I just sit there, the cameraman points the camera at me and that's how I come out."

So she says, "You can do something."

So I said, "What?"

"Give the cameraman a quarter, you'll see the difference," she said.

I think it was Sid Dorfman, a writer I know out on the Coast, who told me about the time he made his first appearance on TV.

All his friends called him afterward to tell him how well he did. The words they used were "witty" . . . "brilliant" . . . "amusing" . . . "funny."

When his mother called all she said was, "Why didn't you wear your blue suit?"

Sid told me about the time he had some friends over for dinner and since they were all involved with TV and movie-making, that's what the dinner conversation was all about.

His mother who had taken no part in this conversation suddenly spoke up and said, "I read in *Variety* that Darryl Zanuck is going into a new production."

Everybody was rather startled by this and especially Sid who had no idea that his mother ever read *Variety*. "I didn't know you even knew who Darryl Zanuck was."

So his mother said to him, "Who doesn't know who Darryl Zanuck is! He's one of the Warner Brothers!"

Six

Cooking Isn't
For Everybody

I have a friend who was telling me that the worst moment in her life was the time she got back from her honeymoon and her husband announced that he had invited his whole family over for dinner.

My friend wasn't much of a cook, while her mother-in-law was famous for family dinners.

This girl was really in a spot. As a matter of fact, as far as she was concerned, defrosting a TV dinner was a challenge. Lighting an oven gave her a trauma. She couldn't even dial Chicken Delight without getting at least three wrong numbers first.

Her talent in the kitchen was limited to mixing martinis and stuffing celery.

She tried talking her husband out of giving this dinner but he kept insisting she was a great cook. He kept reminding her of all the wonderful dinners she had prepared for him when they were going together.

Well, this was no time to start telling him that he always got so blind from her martinis that when he got to the stuffed celery, he thought he was eating a home-cooked meal.

She would just have to give the dinner party.

Naturally, I wanted to know how it came off.

My friend explained.

She went to Doubleday and bought several cookbooks which not only gave complete dinner menus but also recipes and the exact timings for preparation and cooking. Then she went to Scribner's and Brentano's and bought several more. She chose one dinner menu and every day for two weeks when her husband left for work she prepared this dinner.

Her husband never knew what was going on because all traces of her cooking activities disappeared by the time he came home.

For the first four days it disappeared down the incinerator. Then some of it became edible. As more of it became edible, she gifted her cleaning woman, the doorman, elevator operators and the handyman with lunches. Her own lunch put four pounds on her but she didn't care. Her self-image changed from Lauren Bacall to Julia Childs.

The night of her dinner party was also the night of the big power failure in New York. The family couldn't come. She never cooked again.

❧ Why The Weaker Sex Is Weaker

I don't know what it is, but I have found that restaurants are not anxious to cater to lone woman diners.

I've walked into restaurants alone and while I can't say they were exactly hostile, I can say Mao would get a warmer welcome at the Kremlin.

I'm not talking about those restaurants where they serve chicken croquettes. Leftovers I can eat at home.

I'm talking about those classy restaurants where they charge extra for the vegetable.

It so happens I don't have a dainty appetite. I like meat. I especially like the kind of meat dinner you can get in good steak houses. That's where I run into trouble.

Since I'm inclined to approach a possible hassle from a dove's-eye view, I figured out that if I had my dinner before the evening rush, I might find myself in a more conciliatory atmosphere.

I walked into this steak house so early, the hat-check girl hadn't even put out her decoy half dollars to flush out reluctant tippers.

I was standing there alone when the maître d' came over and said, "How many in your party?"

I said, "One."

He said, "There'll be a half-hour wait."

I said, "A half-hour wait. There's nobody in here."

As a matter of fact that restaurant was so empty you could get snow blind from the tablecloths.

"Well," he says, "we're set up for parties of six, four, couples. We're not set up for one."

So I said, "I'm hungry, I'll eat for two."

I know what he's thinking, he's got to seat me, it's the law of the land.

He sat me down in the eastern zone and I sat and sat. I could see all the waiters standing around on the other side of the wall but nobody came near me.

Finally a waiter came over, a defector. He hands me a menu and I said, "Thank you, I don't need the menu. I'd like a steak."

So he tells me how much a steak costs.

I said, "Chance it, maybe I can pay."

In a minute he's back with the whole order. Not that the service was that good. They just wanted me to eat and get out. Just sitting there I was giving the place a bad name.

I started to eat my salad. I didn't have a fork. I

wanted to eat the steak. No knife. They won't allow me sharp instruments. You see, they think if a woman walks into a restaurant alone and pays her own check, if she sees a knife, she'll cut her throat.

I hadn't even finished eating and the waiter is back with the check. They want me out of that restaurant. It's like they're expecting the health inspector and I'm a violation.

No wonder they call us the weaker sex. We never get enough to eat.

Like all wars, this war between restaurants and women loners is based on economics.

Restaurants make their money on liquor—not on the food.

Well, a woman is going to order all the stuff that's too much trouble to make at home. There's very little profit in this.

A man comes into a restaurant alone. Whoopee!!

Naturally he's going to have a couple of drinks before he orders. If he's a regular or they hope to make him one, the bartender buys him a drink on the house. Well, once the house has bought you a drink, you buy the house a drink. Then the house buys you another drink. So you buy the house another drink. After a while you and the house aren't counting but you're both smashed and in love. Who's hungry?

On those drinks and just a handful of peanuts, the restaurant is in business. Who needs some woman coming in to take up space just to eat.

❧ There Are No Secrets From The Butcher

I said to my butcher, "I want a beautiful thick steak for two."

So he says to me, "I'll give you a steak that he'll remember as long as he lives and you too."

"How do you know it's a 'he' coming to dinner?"

"Miss Diamond," he says, "you've been coming in here long enough for me to know that for a 'he' it's steak, for a 'she' you like plump chicken for a chicken casserole."

He was right and I told him so. I had no idea that my butcher was an expert on human behavior ranking up there with Freud, Pavlov and Dear Abby. But he is.

He told me that any butcher can tell from a customer's meat order, what income bracket they're in, how often they entertain and just about everything else that's going on in the family.

A newlywed sticks to anything you can broil or fry. When she gives up frying and starts asking to have the fat cut off everything she broils, you know she's going to have a baby and her doctor has warned her against putting on too much weight. When she stops coming in and starts ordering over the phone you know the baby is due any minute.

Then he told me about a family in the neighborhood whose behavior he could trace through their meat order from the day they first started doing business with him.

The mother paid the bill every two weeks and brought in the husband's pay check to be cashed.

From the check he could see the husband was a city employee.

The meat order ran to hamburger, frankfurters, stew beef and whatever the weekend special was.

When the mother didn't come in she would send one of the kids. There must've been a houseful because they came in all sizes and ages, but all girls.

Suddenly the mother started buying lamb chops. This could only mean one thing. One of the girls brought a fellow home to dinner.

A couple of weeks later there was an order for a large and expensive roast. Obviously the fellow's parents are coming over for dinner.

Suddenly the family stops eating meat. The father is still paying for the wedding.

A couple of months go by during which the family slowly went back to hamburger, frankfurters, stew meat and the weekend special.

In the past few weeks the order remained the same except that they have increased the amount.

This can only mean one thing. The new son-in-law lost his job and the young couple moved in with her folks.

How The South Was Finally Won

You know how people always say, "No matter how well you think you know somebody, there is always something you don't know."

Well, I just found out why people say it. It's true.

I thought I knew my friend Sue as well as anybody could know a friend. And then, sure enough, there was something I didn't know.

Sue had never eaten in a kosher delicatessen.

The very next day, following the evening on which I learned this, I took her to lunch in a kosher delicatessen.

First let me explain that Sue was brought up in the South in an atmosphere of magnolia blossoms, pecan pie, geranium salad and hush puppies.

Inside the kosher delicatessen, the atmosphere is

cooking corned beef, hot pastrami, fat frankfurters, garlic pickles and potato knishes.

From the smile on Sue's face I saw that one whiff in this kosher delicatessen around 1861 would've brought the surrender at Appomattox a lot sooner.

And if you don't know what potato knishes are, it's time you had lunch in a kosher delicatessen. There is more to American food than pizza, chow mein, yogurt and apple pie.

We seated ourselves at a table and when the waiter came over, Sue said, "May we see a menu?"

Before the waiter answered, he turned to the man at the next table eating barley and mushroom soup and said to him, "Must be from uptown."

He turned back to Sue saying, "Lady, I've been a waiter here for twenty years and I've never seen a menu."

So I said to the waiter, "This is her first time in a kosher delicatessen."

Again he turned to the man at the next table who had finished his mushroom and barley soup and was now eating a plate of white radishes, onions and chicken fat and said, "I told you, uptown."

He turned back to me and said, "You're from the moon too or you want to order something?"

"I'll order," I said. I ordered a variety so that my Southern friend could taste several of the foods served in a kosher delicatessen.

". . . And to drink," said the waiter.

"Tea," I said.

He was soon back with the orders and as he placed each one down he addressed us personally by name. "For you, Queen Elizabeth, and for you, Princess Margaret."

Before he got away, Sue said to him, "May I have some milk for my tea?"

"You're eating meat!" he said. "With meat you don't drink milk. There is no milk in this delicatessen for anybody. Senator Javits wouldn't get milk here. This is a kosher delicatessen."

Just then the store cat walked in and got in a cardboard box with her kittens. The kittens started on their lunch.

The waiter saw us watching this and he said to Sue, "They're getting plain tea."

After lunch, as we were walking along the street, a woman came along, recognized me and greeting me by name said, "Miss Diamond, I live on this street, come upstairs I'll make you and your friend coffee."

I said, "Thank you, but we've just had our lunch."

And this darling lady said to me, "I make good coffee. It's not instant. I'll percolate you."

Then she said, "It'll be a treat. I have real sweet cream in the refrigerator."

And Sue said, "Thank you, but we just ate meat!"

☙ How Imperialism Dulled
The English Menu

For years people have been talking about the monotony of English cooking. Not the English. They were so busy that they just ate whatever was put down in front of them.

You know how it is when you live on one continent and your job is on another. It was grab a bite of anything and rush rush rush off to India or Asia or Africa.

Even on the job you couldn't sit down to a proper meal without your houseboy rushing in with a spear in his back yelling, "Sahib Sahib Mau Mau."

Many a Bengal Lancer rode to put down a native uprising with nothing more than copra to chew on for his "elevensies."

Any housewife will tell you that no matter how good a cook she is, it is impossible to keep a roast warm and moist when your husband misses the 5:15 and has to take the 7:15 from the city.

So you can well imagine what it was like all those

years for the English housewife back home when her husband missed the Tuesday boat from Calcutta.

How do you keep a roast warm and moist when having missed the Tuesday boat from Calcutta and he can't get another one until Friday? This one is a local, making all the stops around the Cape of Good Hope to pick up rubber planters who have gone mad mad mad from those native drums beating beating beating.

Quite often there is the extra delay of bringing aboard the bullet-ridden remains of a sugar-plantation owner accompanied by his widow still screaming, "Doesn't it ever stop raining raining raining!"

So you can see now why the English housewife was so devoted to cold mutton.

That's all changed now in England. History has put an end to all that faraway commuting and the telephone company has put an end to all that cold mutton.

You dial a number and you get the recipe of the day. Just as we have dial guideposts for inspiration, they have dial guideposts for dinner.

Just by picking up the phone in England you can get the time, the weather and indigestion.

If a man answers, don't hang up. It's just Chef Milani.

No more coming home to the same old dinner. Unless, of course, you haven't paid your phone bill.

In England nowadays, if your doctor wants you to lose weight, he tells you to cut down on your phone calls.

You can reduce your waistline and your phone bill at the same time.

But what happens now when a wife finds her husband's little black book? Are those telephone numbers blondes, brunettes or favorite recipes?

No matter how he explains it, she'll know something is cooking!

Seven

The Customer Is
Always Wrong

Remember when the customer was always right? From some of the experiences I've had as a customer lately I get the feeling that as soon as I walk into a store I've already made my first mistake.

Now, there's a lamp that I use for reading in bed and the other day when my cleaning woman was in to rearrange the dust, she knocked it over. So I went to buy another lamp to replace it . . . which is a lot easier than trying to replace a cleaning woman.

In the store I picked out a lamp and since the store is in my neighborhood, they told me to expect delivery the next day.

Well, it didn't come the next day or the next day after that or all the next days in the next week.

It was pretty inconvenient being without that reading lamp. I could lose my cleaning woman on account of it.

Without that lamp how is she going to lie on my bed and read? When she comes in for the day you can't expect her to spend the day cleaning.

So I went back to the store to find out what happened to the lamp I bought.

When the salesclerk who sold me the lamp saw me come in, she came over right away because she thought she was going to sell me something else. When I told her I was in to find out about the lamp she had already sold me, she blanked out immediately and looked at me like she had never seen me before.

"I haven't received the lamp," I said.

"Let me check," she said. "I'll be right back."

"Who're you going to check with?" I asked. "I'm the one who didn't receive the lamp."

"Our deliveries are very prompt," she said. "You should've received the lamp by now."

"Take my word," I said. "I don't have the lamp."

Well, she didn't take my word and went back to check. She took so long checking that for a moment I thought she was searching my house and expected to find the lamp hidden there.

Finally she came back triumphant. "I checked. The lamp left the store the day you were in," she said. "It's on the truck."

"When will I get the lamp?" I said.

"It's on the truck, you should get it tomorrow," she said, dismissing me.

Three tomorrows later I went back to the store. "I didn't get the lamp," I said.

"Let me check," she said. "I'll be right back."

"Hold it," I said. "You're checking with me. I did not get the lamp."

"Then it must be on the truck," she said. "I'm sure you'll get it tomorrow."

"I'm not," I said. "Just give me the same model lamp and I'll take it with me now."

"Oh we're all out of that lamp," she said. "That lamp sold twice as fast as any model we've ever carried."

Of course it's selling twice as fast. It's one to a customer and one to the truck.

The bill for that lamp came before the lamp did. Naturally I didn't pay it. Then I started getting reminders from the store's department of accounts about non-payment.

It wasn't until I advised the department of accounts to forward all their correspondence "to the truck" that I got the lamp.

⚘ Don't Love Me—Just Wait On Me

With all the freedom movements we have today, somebody has got to organize and free the American woman from the snobbery of sales people. Especially in some of the better stores.

I've discovered something. If you don't walk in all dressed up like you're going to sit on the dais at a Hadassah luncheon or attend a Balanciaga private showing, they don't pay any attention to you.

The saleslady is always chic. But what's the trick. She works right there in the better dress department and the minute something goes on sale, she's right there and grabs it for herself.

She always has a very elegant hairdo and carries on like I don't know that on her morning off she goes to the Clairol training school and gets the whole thing done for nothing by one of the trainees.

And another thing. You've got to shop when it's convenient for her.

If you come in late in the afternoon, that's inconvenient. She's been on her feet all day and this is the first chance she's had to sit down, and *you* walk in.

Another thing they don't like is if you come in close to closing on Saturday afternoon.

Somehow they've got it figured out that if you walk in late Saturday afternoon you just came in to get a free shopping bag on your way to some discount store where there is a charge for shopping bags. Because if you had any class you'd be home Saturday afternoon resting to go to the country club or a husband-swapping party.

What gets me is how she brings a dress out and holds it against herself . . . at the other end of the store.

Well, often when I'm shopping I'm not wearing my glasses so I'd like to see that blur she's got over there.

I find, when I step forward, she steps backwards. I've learned to make a dash for it.

One time this was happening to me, and I got up close to what she was holding and although it was the middle of winter, she was holding up a lightweight linen dress. So I said to her,

"This is a lightweight linen dress."

So she says, "Of course. Our clients are all shopping for resort wear."

She's putting me in my place, because it's the middle of winter and I'm pale . . . I should be having a love affair with the sun.

So I said to her, "I don't want to see resort wear."

So she says, "That's all we're showing."

And now she gives me, her clients bought this dress

in all different colors and her clients are just mad for this dress and her clients do nothing without her advice and her clients this and her clients that. This nut is a saleslady and she's trying to give me the impression she's a CPA.

I'll never get used to this attitude when I go shopping.

It so happens that I come from a long line of retailers and when a customer came into my father's store, if you bought or not, you were made welcome.

What's more, if I were around, my father would call me in and I would do the Highland Fling. If I was in school, my father would call our dog in and he'd roll over. If my mother was around, you'd get tea and cake.

With all the business I do with Saks Fifth Avenue, I never got tea and cake.

❧ Haute And The French Word For Dressmaker

Like most women I am always looking for new places to shop. And recently, I've become aware of those little dress shops tucked away just off the high-rent shopping districts. To give themselves class, they call themselves "exclusive."

These little dress shops are easily recognizable by their window display.

There is usually one dress in the window. It's not on a figure . . . it's draped on a kitchen chair that has been painted gold. That's what makes it class.

I saw one exclusive shop that didn't even have a dress in the window. There was just a bolt of black chiffon, a picture of Marie Antoinette with her head on and a sign reading "OPEN ALL DAY JULY FOURTEENTH."

These shops never seem busy. The woman in charge usually has a foreign accent and this accent is all part of class.

She is usually some titled countess who has to work for a living, like some Russian countess whose family was ill-advised by Rasputin.

Or it might be some Italian countess with heavy legs.

Sometimes it's the first wife of a famous movie star who dumped her as soon as he became famous.

And you never meet the owner of the place because he's running around to his wife's relatives trying to get a co-signer.

I'm going to try one of these places soon because I want to see what's in there. Why don't you ever see any women in there shopping for dresses?

Are these places really in business to sell dresses or just a front for other activities . . . like maybe a bookie joint. Or is there a speakeasy in back and since nobody goes into the shop in front . . . in back they don't know that prohibition has been repealed.

❧ Never Take An Electric Blanket To The Beach

I bought an electric blanket. I get into bed and I adjust this thing and it gets nice and warm. Then it gets a little warmer and then hot and hotter.

So I thought, well, I have to get used to it. After all, the people who make this thing must know what they're doing.

For the next three nights I slept under this electric blanket that got nice and warm and warmer and then hot and hotter. And all through those three nights I kept dreaming about Smoky the Bear. What kind of dream prince is that!

Then it dawned on me, that blanket is a fire hazard. I don't smoke in bed, but the blanket does.

I took it back to the store where I bought it and the man says to me, "I don't understand this. This blanket was a very good seller and you're the first customer to bring it back with complaints."

Sure I was the first one to bring it back. Obviously his other customers were more particular about the way they appeared in public and were staying indoors until their eyebrows grew back.

I said to him, "I think you ought to do something about this blanket."

He starts examining the blanket more closely and then he says, "Did you take this blanket to the beach?"

I said, "Who takes an electric blanket to the beach? First of all, where am I going to get a cord to reach from my house to Fire Island? Secondly, I wear a bikini and there's no space on a bikini for an outlet."

I had him there so he said, "I'll give you another blanket."

I said, "Okay," because that's what I was there for. And as he goes to get me another blanket he's muttering, "I don't have any more of the one I sold you because it was very popular."

He came back with a blanket and started wrapping it up. So I said, "Let me see it first."

I started examining the blanket and the control seemed very complicated and very different from the one I had before.

"What is that thing?" I asked him.

So he said, "That's a dual control."

Now the only dual control I know, I saw when I was learning to drive and the car the driving instructor brought around had a dual control.

Well, I don't need this in a blanket. It's just going to lay there on my bed. I'm not going to drive it anyplace.

So I said to him, "Look, let's forget it. I'll come back when you get the other blanket in stock again."

So he said to me, "Let me explain this to you. It's not so difficult to understand. This is a 'his and hers' blanket."

It so happens that in my house everything is hers and hers so I took the blanket. I put it on the bed and it really perked up the whole atmosphere. It gave my neighbors something to talk about and it's driving my maid nuts.

The Window Was Just Dressed

Did you ever walk into a store and ask to see something on display in the window?

I once went into a dress shop and asked to see a dress that was on display in the window.

Smiling, the saleslady said, "I can't take it out of the window, the window was just dressed this morning."

So I said, "That's the dress I want to see."

Still smiling (but now she's smiling like I'm Attila the Hun), she said, "We have some other things I could show you."

I said, "No."

I know my rights as an American citizen and I know there is nothing in the Constitution that says she has to take that dress out of the window.

But as an American I can lobby for an amendment to the Constitution. I began to lobby.

I asked to talk to the manager. To the owner. To the buyer. And you know, the democratic process works. They took the dress out of the window.

I go into the fitting room. I put the dress on. I look in the mirror. I HATE THE DRESS. That dress is such a mistake.

If I tell the saleslady that I don't want the dress she's going to kill me.

And she knows she'd get away with it because if there's one window dresser on that jury she'll be acquitted.

I'm thinking: If I buy the dress I'm never going to wear it. I'll just be throwing money away and I'm pretty tight with a buck. So for a moment there, my life is hanging by a thread.

Suddenly the owner of the store comes running in and starts telling me that the dress was sold the evening before and put in the window this morning by mistake. He is contrite . . . and I let him be.

When I got out of that dress and out of that store, a free woman walking in the sun once again, I was thinking: Somebody up there not only likes me but comes down here and goes shopping with me.

Six Cents Off Regular Price

When I watch those television laundry-detergent commercials they don't influence me one bit.

As a matter of fact, when they say their detergent will "put a giant in your washer" they just show his arm. You don't see what the rest of him looks like. How do I know that it isn't the "White Knight" moonlighting.

So when I buy laundry detergent I buy the one that says, "Six Cents Off Regular Price."

As a matter of fact, most women shop that way. It doesn't matter which brand it is, because they're really all the same. It's the "Six Cents Off" that clears the supermarket's shelves.

Anybody could make a fortune with any product if they used as a brand name "Six Cents Off."

And I'll tell you another thing, you don't even need a

product to make a fortune. You could sell empty cans if they're labeled "Six Cents Off."

I buy coffee that way too. Every week another brand of coffee is "ten cents off" so every week I buy a different brand. They're all good and I don't know the difference—and besides, when I'm making coffee, I'm not expecting El Excelente.

I am a great one for keeping stuff in the house for emergencies. Like if there's a big storm and I can't get out or if I have a cold or if I don't have a cold or if it's Monday or if somebody drops in.

If I see a special on lollipops, I buy it. Somebody may drop over with a kid. (I took advantage of a big special on dog biscuits . . . somebody may drop over with a dog.)

Once I passed the gourmet shelf in the supermarket and they were putting a special on whale steaks. Look, you never know when somebody'll drop over with an Eskimo.

They get me another way too. Nothing seems to be priced singly. Especially in the A&P. I never saw anything like it. Everything is 2/23¢ or 4/43¢ or this big special on mixed frozen vegetables . . . 5/97¢. So I buy five boxes. Why should the A&P have the three cents they'll make on me if I buy only the one box I need for twenty cents. Huntington Hartford is rich enough. Why shouldn't I save the three cents and I'll become a patron of the arts.

The only trouble with this is that when I get home with this frozen special, I have no place to put it. My freezer compartment is filled with last week's frozen specials.

So to make room, I decide to defrost a steak and eat home.

I go to work and on my way home somebody invites me out to dinner. Then, after a long leisurely dinner I get home, get ready for bed, open the Frigidaire to get myself a drink of cold water and there it is, this big hunk of wet meat.

Everybody knows that once food is defrosted, you can't refreeze, healthwise. You've got to use it right away.

And I was brought up not to waste food. It was always "Eat . . . people are starving in Europe."

I can't send off this defrosted steak to Europe. I know the Post Office frowns upon this sort of thing.

I do the only thing I can do. I cook it and eat.

I must say I don't enjoy it too much either. First of all I'm sleepy and I just had my dinner.

To avoid this sort of thing which has happened quite often, I took to turning down dinner invitations because I had a steak defrosting at home. I enjoyed this even less.

I decided on a new way to shop. Just buy what you need. No stocking up. If I ran out of butter, that was all I would pick up at the store. In this way, with just one or two items, I could check out at the express check-out counter, enjoy a greater social freedom and no more dinners on dinners.

Except for one thing . . . the express check-out

counter is always longer and slower than the regular check-out counter . . . because the checker at this counter is a trainee and he makes mistakes. So you have to wait until the manager straightens out the mistakes and this takes some time because the manager is chasing three rotten kids from the neighborhood who ran in and grabbed a box of Milky Ways.

Somehow when you're waiting to be checked out, you find yourself looking in the shopping carts of those around you.

I see that the woman in back of me has a bag of the greatest-looking grapefruit I ever saw. Since the line isn't moving anyway, I can go for the grapefruit and not miss my turn.

Just as I pick up the grapefruit, the vegetable man is unpacking a crate of the greatest-looking strawberries I ever saw. Since I only have the butter, grapefruit and two boxes of strawberries, I am still eligible for the express line which still isn't moving.

Then I remember I need garbage-pail bags. Garbage-pail bags are always on the same shelf as the wax paper, aluminum foil, paper towels and facial tissues. Well, these are items that you don't wait until you run out of. You always have extra, just in case.

Then I notice a new item that exactly matches the design of the facial tissues, so I pick up a few rolls.

I now have more than five items so I am no longer eligible for the express line and since I now have to get on the regular check-out line where the items aren't limited I pick up two jars of dry-roasted peanuts and six bottles of sugarless ginger ale.

I look over at the regular check-out counter and that isn't moving either. The cashier is waiting for the manager to come over and okay a customer's check, but the manager is chasing three rotten kids from the neighborhood who ran in and grabbed a box of chocolate-covered cherries and two bags of potato chips.

Now I face it. The monkey on my back is the supermarket. I'll never kick the habit by tapering off with running in for items as I need them. It's got to be complete withdrawal. Luckily I am given the opportunity to dry out. I have to go to the Coast for a couple of weeks which means I'll be living in a hotel room with no kitchen.

There's a dining room in the hotel, a coffee shop and even room service.

But the dining room closes at eleven o'clock. Room service closes after midnight. The coffee shop isn't open until six in the morning.

Suppose I get hungry in the middle of the night?

Luckily I noticed a supermarket not three blocks from my hotel where I can pick up some crackers and cheese, a few apples, and you should see the size of the fresh figs they have out on the Coast. And while I'm in the market I might as well pick up a few packages of that marvelous seasoned flour for fried chicken that you can't find in New York.

✎ My Feet Are Killing Me

I never find buying shoes a problem and I always go along with the changing fashion.

Whatever the style is I go in and buy a pair of shoes. I've worn shoes with a round toe, a square toe, a pointed toe.

And you know something? When I take my shoes off and look at my bare feet, that's what I've got now . . . one round toe, one square toe, one pointed toe and I can't quite make out what all those other things are.

Shoes are made for feet. But whose?

And there's this thing about shoe stores. No matter what shoe store you go into, they always have your size.

Now it so happens that I wear a 7B. But they tell you a 7½A is the same as a 7B. An 8AA is the same as a 7½A. And an 8½AAA is the same as an 8AA.

I have a girl friend who is a head taller than I am, outweighs me by thirty pounds, and we both wear a size 9 shoe.

One spring I walked around in a pair of black patent-leather opera pumps that were stuffed with enough foam rubber to make two non-allergic pillows.

Just this last summer I was intrigued with those transparent shoes that are made out of some kind of plastic stuff. I wore those shoes for a week before I discovered I had the right shoe on the left foot and the left shoe on the right foot.

You'd think that because the shoes are transparent, you could look down and see they're on the wrong feet. Well, you can't. In hot weather those shoes get fogged up.

What gets me is that for over a hundred years foot binding has been outlawed in China. And here we are all walking around with lily feet.

Basic Training For Christmas Shoppers

There is a book out that is the greatest Christmas shopping guide for women that I have ever seen.

I think it's called the Army Basic Training Manual and you can pick it up free at almost any Army Induction Center.

No female Christmas shopper should be without it.

There are tips in there that are invaluable. Like, how you can do your Christmas shopping without getting killed. What to do in face to face combat at officers' parties. . . . I mean office parties.

And there's all kinds of advice on physical fitness so that during the Christmas shopping season, you're in top form to push and shove back.

I learned that the carolers outside the department stores ringing out with Peace On Earth Good Will To Men are camouflage. Inside the stores, the enemy is waiting to attack.

Incidentally, I heard recently that the Vatican is quite concerned about this seasonal belligerency.

And the Ecumenical Council is hoping to come up with some peaceful solutions as soon as final decisions are made about the changes in nuns' habits. Habits in reference to attire . . . not Chaucer.

To give the female Christmas shopper in-training experience of what to expect in the real thing, there are several shopping games in which she must take part. Reading how these shopping games are set up to simulate the conditions of actual Christmas shopping, it seems to me they are equally dangerous.

For example, every Christmas shopping trainee must attend the following year 'round sales.

NATIONALLY ADVERTISED GIRDLES AND BRAS-
SIERES HALF PRICE . . . NOT ALL SIZES IN ALL
COLORS.

LAVISHLY HAND-BEADED SHELLS IMPORTED
FROM HONG KONG DRASTICALLY REDUCED . . .
NOT ALL SIZES IN ALL COLORS.

SUMMER CLEARANCE OF WINTER COATS . . .
SOME FUR TRIMMED . . . MANY WITH NAME
DESIGNER LABELS.

ALL MERCHANDISE MUST GO . . . BUILDING
COMING DOWN.

Attending these sales is only part of what the trainee
is expected to do. She must prove her worth under fire
by having purchased a girdle, a brassiere, a hand-
beaded imported Hong Kong shell, not necessarily her
size, and a winter coat, not necessarily fur trimmed.

When these exercises have been accomplished there
is still the final and severest shopping game. This final
test divides the trainees into those who are really going
to be fit for Christmas shopping and those who will be
advised to stay out of the stores and just send their
friends Christmas Candygrams.

I know I could never pass this final test. The one
called . . .

NATIONALLY   ADVERTISED   COMBINATION
WASHER AND DRYER MACHINES AS SEEN ON TEL-
EVISION 44¢. . . . FREE TO THE FIRST THREE
CUSTOMERS.

When the trainee has been one of the first three cus-tomers, three times, she is not only a Christmas shopper her country can be proud of but the owner of three Na-tionally Advertised Combination Washer and Dryer Machines As Seen On Television.

As we all know, for the Christmas shopping season the stores usually restrict one area of the store for male shoppers only. For him they reproduce an atmosphere of bacchanalia in which he is plied with spirits and real live girls while the female shopper is lucky if the water fountain near the elevators is working.

Naturally there is a flare-up of envy. You might even contemplate changing your sex. Don't . . . unless of course your analyst has already advised it.

Only 364 Shopping Days Left Till Christmas

With me it's not only Christmas shopping but Chanukah present giving too, so at that time of the year I have interfaith expenses.

And since they both come around the same time of year, you have to be very careful when mailing.

Never send a Chanukah present to Israel marked "Do Not Open Until Christmas."

What gets me is how the stores in New York know the exact psychological approach to put their customers into a super-buying mood.

Like when you pass Saks Fifth Avenue, they have a chorus of angels singing "Come All Ye Faithful."

And down on Thirty-fourth Street, Macy's has a recording of angels singing "Come All Ye Thrifty."

And in front of the discount houses it's just a man with a megaphone yelling "Come and Get It."

And this works. I must say every time I hear those angels singing in front of Saks Fifth Avenue, I'm right in the mood to do some more shopping.

Except that after the angels in front of Saks Fifth Avenue put me in the mood I always feel guilty shopping at Macy's.

Of course there are problems Christmas shopping and one of them is shopping for my married friends.

I find they're married one Christmas and the next Christmas they're not.

The only couple I know in the last few years who were faithful to their marriage was Bonnie and Clyde. But that didn't do me much good because they weren't on my Christmas list. Come to think of it, I don't think they were on anybody's Christmas list . . . because they weren't around until Christmas.

Huntley and Brinkley seem to be sticking it out as a couple from Christmas to Christmas. But even here, who can tell? You know how people talk and lately when one announces the other is off on some special assignment, rumors start flying around that he isn't off on a special assignment at all but that he's been seen over at the other network having lunch with Walter Cronkite.

I now find that the safest way to approach gift giving to couples is to wait until the last moment . . . and I don't have anything monogrammed with their initials . . . if I do have anything monogrammed I just have them embroider "To whom it may concern."

It isn't easy keeping a gift list for kids from year to year.

Now there's one little girl I know who started a collection of dolls of all nations. All she ever wanted for Christmas was another doll to add to her collection.

Now this is a kid who is still shy of her teens. Well, I can just tell you this, before she had even collected the dolls of the North Alliance countries, she gave up the whole project and shacked up in Greenwich Village with an ex-boy scout from Westchester where they spend all their time covering each other from head to toe with giant amaryllis cut from Burpee Seed Catalogues.

But there is one list that never changes and the most important man in my life naturally heads the list. The handyman.

In the country it's the man with the hoe but in the city it's the man with the plunger.

Forget the handyman at Christmas and for the rest

of the year he forgets you, and you're in big trouble when your sink begins to leak.

I have a friend who once forgot the handyman and the next time the plumbing backed up, by the time the handyman came up she was going down for the third time.

You should've seen her place . . . three-and-one-half rooms of kelp.

Naturally she had an awful maid problem. Where are you going to find anybody who can dust and tread water?

And what happened to my friend is not unusual. I don't have to tell you what happened when Noah forgot to take care of his handyman at Christmas and his sink began to leak.

Another person on my permanent Christmas list is the manicurist. I'd never forget her, especially when I think how defenseless I am while she's armed with those sharp cuticle scissors.

I must say when the doorman where I live puts up the Christmas tree in the lobby, he has the same friendly smile for those who have remembered him at Christmas and those who have not.

Except that when he trims the tree, if you have not there you are on the tree, hanging in effigy.

Believe me, there's more to Christmas giving than the spirit of Christmas. It's also a matter of survival.

Eight

Happy New Year, I Think!

I always approach New Year's Eve with great trepidation.

Because one year I was at a party right before New Year's Eve and I met a new man. I don't mean a humanoid, he was an earthling.

It's just that he was new to me.

He invited me out for New Year's. I thought, why not? After all, a new man, a new year, new action.

He interested me.

We got to talking at the party and he told me he was a doctor and that he was planning to specialize in orthopedics. Now it so happens I have a bad back, so al-

ready there's a physical attraction and mutual interests.
My bad back.

So I said, "Okay, I'll go."

A week before New Year's Eve he called me up and
he said, "The party we're going to is rather late, so I'll
pick you up about 11 o'clock."

I said, "Okay, just buzz me when you get to my house
and I'll come down."

When I go out with somebody for the first time, I
don't want him in the house.

It's always the same. He'll walk in, look around and
say, "Oh, you live here alone?"

Then he establishes a beachhead on the sofa and
says, "It's so restful here. Do we have to go out?"

I have a small apartment, so wherever I'm sitting I'm
directly within his firing line.

Now who needs this? I didn't wash my hair in the
middle of the week to engage in active combat.

At 11 o'clock on New Year's Eve my date buzzes me
and I come down.

Just as we start out he says, "I hope you don't mind,
I have to make a house call."

Well, what'm I going to say? Of course I said, "I
don't mind."

We're going out for the first time. So you have to be
warm and lovable. Later, when you get to know him,
you can open a big mouth.

I waited in the car while he made his house call. It
didn't take long, about fifteen minutes, and when he
came out he said, "You know it's New Year's Eve.

There may be some emergencies, I better call my service."

Well, of course there were emergencies. It's New Year's Eve! There have been all kinds of office parties; people are getting looped. They're ready for the stomach pump. For me, so far, it's a safe and sane Fourth of July.

On the car radio I hear Guy Lombardo playing Old Lang Syne.

So I wish General Motors a Happy New Year and I kiss the car.

I must say this was the first time I ever necked with a car. Believe me, it's nothing.

Now I'm sitting there and it's getting pretty warm, so I decide to turn down the heater.

Well, this was a car with which I wasn't too familiar and it has a lot of buttons and knobs and levers with which I wasn't too familiar.

I start pushing and pulling and getting nowhere.

I keep on trying some more. Believe me, if this car had been an organ I would be playing The Star Spangled Banner.

Finally I hit something that I thought was the heater. But in some cars the air conditioning is connected with the heater, and when I hit this thing, it got so cold in that car, I went out in the snow to warm up.

It's New Year's Eve and I'm all dressed up standing out in the snow. My shoes don't have any front or back and my dress doesn't have any front or back.

By the time the doctor came out I was shivering.

He took one look at me and said, "I better take you back to your apartment and put you to bed."

Which was perfectly respectable. Now that I have a chill, I'm not his date, I'm his patient.

When we got back to the house, he gave me a shot of something and I shaped up fine the next day.

I must say, he's a good doctor, but a rotten date.

My Doctor Is A Hypochondriac

There are some people who call the doctor for every little ache and pain. I don't.

I always feel that I would be taking his time away from somebody who is sicker than I am. And I'm right, because the person sicker than I am is my doctor.

I'm not a hypochondriac, but my doctor is.

I called him one night and I said to him, "I feel terrible, you've got to tell me what to do."

So he mumbles something.

I said to him, "I don't understand what you're saying."

Now, he repeats his mumble.

So I said, "I really don't understand what you're saying. What've you got in your mouth?"

"My thermometer," he says.

"I don't feel well," I said. "I've got awful chills and fever."

So he says, "102° temperature . . . that's serious."

I said, "I don't have a 102° temperature."

So he says, "I have."

I told him to take two aspirin, drink plenty of liquids and not to bother to come out to see me but stay in bed and get plenty of rest.

You know, he called me the next day and told me how much better he was feeling. It was most gratifying. When he hung up, for a moment there, I felt that I had the eye of an eagle and the hand of a woman.

A lot of doctors are like that. They identify with their patients.

When I go to my doctor with hives, I haven't left the office yet and he's scratching.

Can you imagine the madness if a male gynecologist identified with his patients. I'd like to be around the day some female patient walks in for a rabbit test and it comes back positive. He'll go crazy, or even worse if he's not married.

Say What You Want About Doctors

Appeared in *Cosmopolitan,* June, 1966

I really never thought much about doctors one way or the other most of my life, until I was over in Italy last summer visiting with some friends who have a cottage in Lido Beach, Venice. Actually, I didn't think about them then but something happened to me there that got me to thinking about them almost exclusively after I got home. At the time, however, there I was on the beach in Venice and it was almost impossible to think about anything but the Italian men.

Now I have an open mind about whether it was Columbus or the Vikings who first landed in America, but looking at these tall, blond, northern Italians, I was convinced the Vikings not only landed in Italy sometime in their careers, they must also have landed the Italian women. Their great, great, great, great, great, great male grandchildren, my beach playmates, all looked like Burt Lancaster. It was amazing how they could communicate with an American girl with just the tiniest English vocabulary. Those blond Italian men may only have known five words but each one had a motel of meaning. They could manage to convey, "You Jane . . . me Tarzan," with just a couple of Adriatic grunts.

I don't mind telling you this continental approach got me, especially after the approach at Jones Beach which is usually, "What kind of sandwiches did you bring?" Naturally I got myself a bikini. Any girl knows when you're pushing merchandise, packaging is important. Then I began romping on the beach. Let's face it, when you're in a bikini and there's a Burt Lancaster for every hour of the day, you don't drag your feet. Unmindful of the physical hazards, I plunged into the fun and games with muscles that I had put in drydock at the cessation of our hostilities with the Japanese.

I guess I should have known better than to send my mothball fleet into active combat. The morning I got up to fly back to New York, I discovered I was stiff . . . but really stiff. I was alive, yes, but rigor mortis had set in. I couldn't bend anything and there are several things in your body that have to bend so you can sit down.

So with legs as limber as two stalks of frozen broccoli, I stood to eat my last breakfast—in Italy, I mean. Then I stood on the launch taking me to the airport and I stood on the plane from Italy to France. Everything hurt—which maybe made parting from the North

Italian men less painful than it might have been. I couldn't think about anything but my joints. When I got to the airport in France I still couldn't bend anything, but I only knew I was in real trouble when I lost all interest in earthly goods. There I was in a duty-free airport. The stuff on sale was going at a bigger discount than you could get at Korvette's and I didn't buy anything. When a woman doesn't feel like shopping, she's had it.

Thanks to the solicitude of Pan American who bedded me down on two seats, I didn't stand from France to New York. I didn't sit either; I just lay there kind of like an ironing board. As we neared New York, the stewardess offered to radio ahead to have my doctor waiting, but I knew better than that. It was a hot summer weekend, and on that kind of weekend where are you going to get a doctor in New York? They're all stuck on the road driving between Park Avenue and Grossinger's. The airline did get an ambulance to take me home and I must say the ambulance attendants were wonderful. They carried me off the plane. They carried me into my apartment and what's more they carried me onto my bed. But this is as far as the ambulance attendants carry you. Also, at this point they don't leave without being paid. How's that for a cash-and-carry business?

About this time I decided I'd have to try to get a doctor and that's when I began thinking about them seriously after all those years. If I'd known the kind of foolishness I'd shortly become involved in by calling any doctor, I would've called Buddy Hackett. I'd still be suffering but at least I'd be laughing.

I racked my brains for who to call. There was a doctor who'd been taking care of me when I was living in California, but there was no point in calling him. If you can't get a doctor in New York to come crosstown, you can't expect a doctor in California to come cross-country. I also knew a doctor living close by who was dating me, but if I called him professionally I could foul up the whole relationship. Besides, if he found me in bed he might think I was pushing.

Finally I decided to call a doctor in whom I had complete confidence. At the beginning of last winter this doctor had given me a series of preventative cold shots. And all winter, as I caught one cold after the other, his unfailing advice to take two aspirin, drink plenty of liquids and stay in bed, did cure me, I must admit.

When I called this doctor, he came as quickly as possible. He gave me a complete examination, but really complete, down to reading the inscription on my ankle bracelet and observing from the design of my summer tan that I had worn a bikini. Before he left, he called the drugstore and ordered two prescriptions to be delivered at once.

In all fairness to the doctor, I must say that in less than two hours, after taking the medicines he prescribed, there were results. From the pink capsules I broke out into a rash and from the little white pills I developed swelling. But I still couldn't bend the proper body parts without a great deal of pain. When I called the doctor to tell him of the unwelcome side effects of the pills, I could see he was right on the ball. Quick as anything he said, "Don't take them anymore."

For the next three days he showed up every morning, ordered new medication on the phone from the drugstore and was out of the house—all without his feet ever touching the ground. And every afternoon I would call him, to tell him about the new rash, the new swelling and the old pain.

The next couple of days I didn't see Dr. Twinkletoes at all; he just called the drugstore from his office. Then it was the weekend again and in my neighborhood the drugstores are closed on Sunday, so of course there was really no reason for my doctor to stay in town. (That's another thing—neighborhood drugstores close on Sunday. I often think that one tsetse fly making a wrong turn from South Africa could wipe out all of Manhattan before the drugstores opened on Monday.)

By Monday not only had my bikini tan faded but I noticed that when I tried to get out of bed I was no longer casting a shadow. At this point Twinkletoes sprang into action. From his tutoring, I learned that this is the age of specialization in medicine and the function of the general practitioner is as a sending station. He has a list of specialists to whom he sends you. Specialists are trained in separate parts of the body.

Unfortunately, as it later turned out in my case, when I brought a specialist my parts of the body all put together he was stumped.

Anyway, Twinkletoes told me he was sending me to a specialist who was best in his field, whatever his field was, and he arranged an appointment. Meanwhile, I still couldn't bend anything and I was still suffering. Since specialists don't make house calls and since this was just the first in a series of specialists I was to see, I spent more time on my back in ambulances during this period than Oscar Levant. Unbending in my pain, I was flipped from one stretcher to another.

When I arrived at the office of the first specialist, I learned that he was in Europe, boning up on his specialty, and that his practice was being taken over by his summer replacement. This was the case with all the specialists recommended to me; in each office I found a summer replacement—just like on television. For somebody like me, who works in television, this is not reassuring. We know about summer replacements and we know very few of them ever make it in prime time.

Now one of the reasons the general practitioner sends his patient to a specialist is to get the benefit of more than one opinion. I not only got more than one opinion, I got a range of opinions as varied as Howard Johnson's ice cream flavors. At first this confused me. But in practice it actually effected my cure. One of the opinions I got was that I stay off my feet and in bed. Another of the opinions was for me to get out of bed and go about my business. And that's the "more than one opinion" that pulled me through. During the day I got out of bed to go about my business and during the night I stayed off my feet in bed.

It is not only important to get more than one opinion, you see, but even more important that the opinions do not concur.

In spite of my experience with some of today's doctors I suppose it could be said in their defense that . . . that . . . how about it . . . ifff . or it could be said . . . on the other hand . . . or . . . or . . . You know, I really can't think of anything that could be said.

You Exercise And I'll Watch

I walk into a health food store once in a while to browse around and I'm often tempted to buy some of that health food. But instead of just selling it to you, they start explaining how it's fertilized. That always throws me off.

One thing about the A&P, I buy the food and take my chances.

But I always pick up and read the pamphlets they give away free in health food stores.

One I read listed all the foods being consumed in this country which are shortening the lives of all of us.

I had copies made and sent them to all the reactionaries in the Senate. I wanted them to see what a waste of time it is fighting old age security legislation since none of us are going to live long enough to collect any of it.

There is also a list of all the foods that are good for you . . . ecch!

And they always have pictures of people bragging about what health foods did for them. Not one female could hold a calorie to Sophia Loren.

Sophia Loren was brought up on Neapolitan pasta. Who's going to believe starchy foods aren't good for you when you just have to look at Sophia Loren and see she's busting with good health.

There was also a picture of a woman who could sit on her hair. She claimed this luxurious growth was the result of a health food diet. Well, I'm not giving up veal parmigiana to sit around on my hair.

But I try to keep an open mind about health foods because an awful lot of people go for it.

One day while I was browsing around in a health food store I bumped into a girl I went to school with who was loaded down with her purchases.

She had changed so much since we went to school together that I barely recognized her. She gave all the credit to eating health foods.

I was really impressed when she told me how popular she now was with men. By July 4th, she told me, she already was booked for New Year's Eve.

I went right over to the counter and bought two pounds of organic sunflower seeds . . . and the heck with how these sunflowers were fertilized. Because this girl would never have gotten to a class dance if the rest of us didn't draft, threaten and bribe brothers, cousins and the class homosexual to escort her.

All the girls liked her. Of course we all liked her. What girls don't like a girl who is no threat?

By the time we got to our last year in school and our last school dance we had exhausted all possible sources to get her a date. It was then that we did the impossible.

We actually brainwashed a foreign exchange student whose religious beliefs prohibited the two sexes dancing together. When we got them to the dance he chickened out and wouldn't dance with her. But it was still a victory. At least she wasn't sitting out the dances alone.

And this is the girl who was now telling me she had no social problems at all.

While she was talking I noticed that since we were in school she must've dropped forty pounds. Her over-bite was gone so she must've had her teeth capped. I kept staring at her, so she told me she had had her nose fixed and was wearing contact lenses.

When I got home I discovered that I must've left my two pounds of sunflower seeds on the bus. I didn't care.

I remembered that her father ran a very large wholesale dairy business. Being in the dairy business he's dealing in products with a pretty high fat content not to mention the cholesterol. Well, it's the healthy food like this that made the healthy money it takes to cap teeth, have your nose fixed and be fitted for contact lenses.

Once I heard a health addict on TV discuss his monodiet of only grass. I was fascinated; all the time he was talking about eating nothing but grass, I kept wondering if he gives milk.

Can you imagine what happens when he takes his girl to the park? She thinks he wants to neck. What he wants is to graze.

There are some advantages to marrying a fellow on a grass diet.

You not only won't have to spend any time in the kitchen, you'll have the neatest lawn in the neighborhood.

Of course you'll have to keep your eye on the widow across the street who never bothered to get a lawn mower and instead just keeps borrowing your husband.

Health addicts carry on about exercise too. And there are pamphlets and books that I browse through free.

They're all pretty much the same except for a new one that's just come out based on the theory that exercise done in the company of a member of the opposite sex is more stimulating. I agree with that. Anything done in the company of a member of the opposite sex is more stimulating.

The author of this book is shown illustrating her

method of physical fitness with a very cute fellow. From some of the illustrations I can see why exercising this way is more stimulating. It's also very friendly.

Whoever thought muscle tone would become a sex symbol!

I used to exercise a lot but I gave it up. I've found that, for me, anything more strenuous than sitting is a physical hazard.

I've tried swimming, diving, golf, tennis, handball, the works. And every time I've tried it, I've sprained something, pulled something, bent and broken something.

There was always a part of me wrapped in bandages, hidden in splints or covered by casts. It wasn't until I gave the whole thing up forever that I could look in the mirror and see myself completely assembled.

I know physical fitness is important but with me it became a question of physical fitness or survival.

I also know that you've got to do something to keep your system in condition and your blood circulating. My problem was how to keep my blood moving without spilling any.

I worked it out. I have a vibrator in my bed. In this way, the bed exercises and it's great for me because when I fall out of bed, I just climb back in and I'm exactly where I should be when the doctor comes.

Why Single Girls' Colds Last Longer

I've discovered something. When you're single it takes twice as long to get rid of a cold than it would if you're married. Really. I'll tell you why.

Now I had this terrible cold and a friend of mine calls up and invites me out to dinner. So I said, "I can't go out. I've got this terrible cold and I'm in bed."

So he says, "Well then, I'll come over and see you."

Well, now, if a fellow is coming over, you can't sit around in the flannel bathrobe with the binding hanging.

You've got to get out of bed and put on that thin thing you got for Christmas with the ribbons hanging.

Well, those things are drafty.

Now if you're married, you can sit around like a slob, keep warm and get rid of the cold.

Nine

The Wild Blue Yonder Is Getting Wilder

I travel by plane a lot but I'm really chicken about flying. As a matter of fact, when I step off a plane, I always feel that I've won a bet.

As for all the work that's being put into increasing the speed of planes in the future, they don't have to bother on my account. I'm never in that much of a hurry to get where I'm going. And if the plane isn't going to get there, I certainly am in no hurry.

Naturally, I was quite shaken when I came across a

book called "The Drinking Man's Diet." This diet is for drinking men who can lose weight without giving up drinking. What's more, according to the book, this diet was started by Air Force pilots. For a while there, I wouldn't get on a plane until I smelled the pilot's breath.

I'm not too thrilled about the airlines calling in high-fashion designers to outfit the stewardesses with changes of costume. They insist that it's all part of making my flight more comfortable. It so happens that when I travel, I get pretty crumpled. Now what comfort is it to me, sitting there like a slob, to see that stewardess walking around all gussied up.

And if something I'm wearing suddenly snaps, breaks or tears and I'm in need of temporary repairs, I'd like to know how you ask one of the ten best-dressed women if she's got a safety pin.

What gets me is how the airlines have done nothing new with the life jacket they expect me to wear in case we ditch. No wonder they keep that awful-looking thing out of sight under the seats.

I suppose these costume changes on the stewardesses are a comfort to the male passengers when she comes around asking, "Coffee, tea or would you please zip me up?"

I just hope nobody gets the idea of having the pilot keep changing his outfit while we're in flight.

That's all I need. Just as we're getting ready to land, the pilot's zipper gets stuck.

❧ The Original Traveling Salesman Story

I met a lovely lady visiting this country from her native India.

Whenever I meet a lady from India my first impulse is to ask them to take off their sari so that I can see how they fix it to stay on. I can't.

One birthday somebody gave me a sari with printed instructions enclosed, but I can't seem to make it. Indian ladies don't use safety pins. Even though I know it's cheating it's the only way I can keep mine up and around. Scotch tape does a good job but in a very warm room it begins to itch, so I never bothered to write the company to tell them there are really 102 uses for their product.

And from a former Bengal Lancer I learned that it would not be wise to suggest to an Indian lady that she take off her sari so I can see how they fix it to stay up. It seems that if his regiment had not had this same curiosity about saris, England would not have lost India. To tell the truth, I always thought those Bengal Lancers were too fresh.

Since this Indian lady was in this country extending her studies in nuclear physics I decided not to ask her anything as frivolous as how her sari stays up.

Foreign women are inclined to think of us as pampered superficial dolls. They've forgotten how many fine riveters we developed in World War II, and at what a price. Once a muscle always a muscle. What riveting has done, no Revlon body contour salon can undo.

Since my muscles aren't too impressive I figured I'd floor her with my intellectual power. I asked her if multiple marriages still exist in India.

She told me that while most Indians are progressing along Western ways, there are some in remote areas who still retain the customs of hundreds of years past. In these remote areas, multiple marriages still exist.

For example, a tradesman gets married. His business may take him to another village miles and miles away. Since he travels by camel, reaching this other village may take him a whole year. In such a case, it is not unusual for him to have a wife here too.

This makes sense to me. If a man has been on the desert for a year, eating in those oasis diners, he must be pretty tired of those gritty cous-cous burgers. You can't blame him for wanting a home-cooked meal.

After he leaves Wife Number Two, his next business stop may take him another year. "Loving Arms" Number Three awaits him there with a hot meal. An Indian tradesman with an expanding business and a sucker for home cooking can have four wives. It's a great setup for him but what about the four wives?

Here are four housewives with an awful lot of spare time on their hands. Even without one kitchen appliance it doesn't take a whole year to cook one hot dinner. I'd like to see Dr. Joyce Brothers cope with this kind of unfulfilled housewife.

Are they boning up to get their high school equivalency diploma? Sitting around getting loaded?

Spending those long days making a whole animal menagerie with a Magic Daisy Winder?

It so happens they haven't got any spare time. They're busy all day taking care of their kids.

You see, even in the remotest parts of India, no husband would be so crude as to eat and run.

❧ The Nouveau Poor

I got to thinking about the British Royal Family the other day. They are supported by the government. That family is really on welfare. Even the place they live in belongs to the government. Buckingham Palace is a public housing project. I've heard that they do have a little income property. I hope so. Who can live on those welfare checks?

"You've got to admire the way the British Royal Family makes "do" with what they have. What other family do you see on the freeway today in a horse and carriage!

Remember Queen Elizabeth's Coronation; how proudly she stood in the coronation robes. Everybody knows those coronation robes are hand-me-downs.

She must be a wonderful mother.

Look at the sacrifices she makes so that her children are always dressed nice. I've seen pictures of her in uniform reviewing her regiment. How many mothers do you know who would have their picture taken wearing army shoes?

As if Queen Elizabeth doesn't have enough worries. Now she's got to start worrying about marrying off her daughter.

Did you know that the European market is flooded with unmarried royalty?

There was a time when a prince married a princess and lived happily ever after. And why not! His family had money. Her family had money.

In those days a prince could be a high school dropout and get any high-salaried executive spot in the Kingdom. And he didn't have to go through a whole series of preliminary aptitude sessions with the Kingdom's psychologists. Neither did his wife, the princess.

They could both be rotten, cold, anti-social personalities and he still got the job. All he had to do was ask his father.

I'll tell you another thing. These princes had no qualms about trading in on the family's name. They didn't even bother to change their names so that maybe the people they work with would think they got the job on merit. Not them. If the father's name was Louis I, the son's name was Louis II, and his son's name was Louis III . . . unless the father's name was Charles I then the son's name would be Charles II. They really ran nepotism into the ground.

This went on for hundreds of years. It was so unfair. I can't tell you how many high school graduates who were next in line for top executive positions were passed over for some prince, just because his father, the King, owned the company.

Well, what can I tell you. This is no way to run a business. Plant after plant started closing down. People were thrown out of work. Money became very tight.

That is, money became very tight for the man in the street. Royalty had it all. But they wouldn't admit it.

Suddenly a French CPA by the name of Robespierre opened a big mouth and demanded that his king show him his books. The king tried to stall Robespierre because there weren't any books. What king keeps books? A king charges everything he buys. What king pays bills?

Do I have to tell you what happens when you tell a CPA you don't keep books.

When George, a king in England, heard about this he started putting taxes on everything so he could have a set of books to show his accountant. But it was too late. He stayed king but he lost a lot of income from his thirteen colonies, and eventually the thirteen colonies.

Accountants all over the world began taking over. Right and left kings and czars were kicked out, and replaced by anybody who could keep books.

And that's why the European market is flooded with unmarried royalty. Nobody wants to marry an unemployed prince . . . and unemployed princes can't afford to get married.

I'll never forget how upset the Queen of the Netherlands was when her daughter, Irene, married a Spanish prince.

And I can understand it. After all, a queen is a mother. Some of them are even named "The Queen Mother." They take being a mother seriously.

A queen raises a daughter like a princess. Everything the best. So when her daughter marries, she wants the best for her: a doctor, a lawyer, a computer operator.

What business opportunities are open to a Spanish prince? Experienced kings are out of work.

Princess Irene married her prince and said she's going to live in Spain with him and work to make him king.

Now there's nothing wrong with a wife working after she's married until her husband is established in his profession. So she works and makes him king. Okay, he's a king. How is he going to support a wife?

Who needs kings today? We need schoolteachers.

And the few kingdoms that are around today aren't passing out any jobs. They've got their own sons-in-law to take into the business.

And the new countries starting up don't need kings. They need schoolteachers.

If the prince would just stop dreaming and look around at the way things are today he'd see that IBM isn't sending representatives to Harvard to recruit kings.

The smart thing for him to do is become a photographer. There's very good money in photography for anybody with his kind of connections. There's a photographer in England whose wife was a princess when he married her and he's making a very nice living for her.

Royalty believe in large families. And from just taking pictures of his wife's relatives he's built a nice trade.

Hotel Living And Why It Isn't

I thought my problems with hotel living were over when I no longer could only afford to stay in six-dollar rooms.

You know those rooms. They give you one towel a week. The maid shows up twice a week to rearrange the dust and hangs around the lobby the rest of the week to make sure you don't check out without leaving her tip.

Naturally, this does not include the YWCA where according to what they have to say about themselves on TV, they not only offer neat, inexpensive, clean rooms but a plethora of educational and recreational facilities thrown in. What's more, the YWCA more than suggests that this mingling of residents and even non-residents produces a trauma-free atmosphere in which personality development is a cinch.

How about that? A clean, inexpensive, neat room and personality development. It's like having Dr. Rose Franzblau at your beck and call night and day.

The YWCA is beginning to sound pretty attractive to me since I have just crossed the country stopping in first-class hotels and finding a never-ending trauma-full atmosphere where I often had great need for a resident psychiatrist. No only wasn't my personality developing but I became a pitiful cowering shell under the despotism of hotel management.

Now you take the resort hotels which charge the same for single or double occupancy.

This could be the result of a romantic optimism shared by the management and the single who checks in single and expects to check out double. Since I check in single and check out single, I'm not sure if the management is a romantic optimist or an incurable peeping Tom.

Now I wonder, will he spread the word that I

checked in single and checked out single or is the double-occupancy rate I paid the bribe the management is exacting to keep his mouth shut?

It seems to me that the resort hotels would do well to place next to the Gideon Bible a copy of anything written by Helen Gurley Brown.

Another thing I learned to avoid on my trip is any hotel that promises "a home away from home."

It was at one of these hotels that there was no phone by the bed. There was a phone but it was way over on the other side of the room. This struck me as rather unusual since in most first-class hotels there is not only a phone by the bed to call room service but a phone near the TV to call about the TV not working. There's even a phone in the bathroom which I imagine is to call for help!

As far as I'm concerned any hotel that offers room service doesn't mean it if there isn't a phone by the bed. Because I'm not getting out of bed until breakfast comes.

It's convenient for me to have the phone by the bed so I can call in about an hour to find out what's holding it up and then call again after that and sometimes even again. What's even more important about having a phone by the bed is that when it looks as if breakfast will be up for lunch, I can call the drugstore and have them send something that'll tide me over until lunch when I'll have the breakfast I ordered from room service originally.

Another reason I don't get out of bed until my breakfast comes is that I'm not too happy about hotel waiters. I mean the way they walk into the room. Sure they knock first, but if I get out of bed before breakfast has arrived and I'm under the shower, I don't hear the knock. When I come out of the shower to get my underwear laid out on the bed, who do you think is standing there?

What do you say to a waiter when you're stark naked? All I can think of is "hello."

So you can understand that when I reached over for the phone by the bed and it wasn't there, I wasn't too happy.

On my way out that morning I stopped by and asked the manager to move the phone.

He said that they no longer put phones by the bed because guests sitting on the bed to use the phone caused wear and tear on the mattress.

I could see that this hotel was really a home away from home. My mother never let me have a phone by my bed either—for exactly the same reason.

I never stood up to my mother because she made great apple pie but since I never heard of anybody going to war to fight for hotel apple pie, it wasn't un-American of me to stand up to a hotel manager.

I won a battle but he won the war. He agreed to move the phone for a ten-dollar charge.

This extra charge of ten dollars in addition to the rate of my room got me to thinking.

Since my room was on the twelfth floor and I had no intention of walking up and down twelve flights of stairs, was I going to be charged for the wear and tear on the elevator cables every time I used the elevator?

Another thing that began to bother me was the cost of electrical wiring. I often read late into the night. Was this hotel monitoring the hours I used the bed lamp? My mother did.

I moved to a hotel that had a phone by the bed. I spent a merry week talking on the phone and wearing out the mattress and the wiring. When I checked out I took an ashtray, all the stationery in the desk, the memo pad and pencil by the bed and a single-rose vase. Not only didn't the management seem to mind, they hoped I'd come back the next time I was around that way. I will.

Most first-class hotels don't allow cooking in the room which is fine with me because I always travel with an electrical immerser and a little instant coffee. Hotels call this cooking in the room. I call it survival until room service comes.

What I usually do when I have my first meal from room service is take the cup and saucer and hide it.

You see, if I leave it around where the maid can see it, she's going to remove it. I don't have to tell you, she's for management.

But no matter where I hide it, she finds it.

I have taped it under the mattress. I have put it inside the television set. Once I removed the tubes from the radio and put the cup and saucer in there. She found it.

I don't bother hiding it in the chandelier or hanging it outside the window because they know all about that. If they're too young to have seen Ray Milland hide his bottle in "Lost Weekend" when it first played in theaters, they've seen it rerun on television . . . so that's the first place they look.

I have really run out of hiding places. I'm convinced there isn't a hotel maid anywhere in this country who doesn't know where Judge Crater is. The only reason they haven't turned him in is because he's a big tipper.

But don't think I'm not up to meeting the challenge the maid presents. What I do now when I check out is hide her tip. She'll find it, but it'll be awfully wet.

I have had my moments of travail in hotel lobbies too.

I was traveling to the West Coast with the producer and the director of a TV special I was writing.

The network had arranged accommodations for all of us at the same hotel. When we got there, the producer and the director went over to the desk to check us in.

"Get me some cash," I called after them.

Since this was a business trip, I was on an expense account with the producer's company. Why should I use my own money?

While I was standing in the lobby waiting for them to check us in and bring me some money, a priest came over to me.

He introduced himself and said, "I had to come over to speak to you and to tell you how much my mother enjoys watching you on television."

Then he said, "I know you're not of my faith but while you're in this city perhaps you could visit my church. My mother and her ladies' group would be delighted if you would."

This kind of got to me and while I'm standing there with the priest, the producer and the director walk right over to me and the producer starts counting out fifty dollars.

He doesn't pay any attention to the priest. All he's got on his mind is the TV special we have to do and he wants to get started.

He hands me the fifty dollars and says, "To make it convenient and to save time, I've gotten us all rooms on the same floor."

I'm thinking fast to clear things up with the priest but that producer is talking faster and now he says, "Do you want us to come to your room or do you want to come to ours?"

As I followed them toward the elevators I was thinking what a blow had just been dealt to interfaith relationships.

❧ *Europe Is A Fun City*

Whenever people I know talk about going to the Continent for the first time, I always tell them to learn the language of the country they're planning to visit.

The first time I went to Paris, I didn't. I should have. Because I went into a phone booth on a street corner to make a phone call and it wasn't a phone booth.

Incidentally, in Paris and in many continental cities there are public comfort stations all over the place for both men and women. And that's exactly what I discovered once looking for some comfort. They are for both men and women. The same one, I mean.

It takes a little getting used to. Come to think of it, it took me a lot of getting used to. What'm I kidding around for, I'll never get used to it.

How can any American get used to it? If you're in there and the attendant is stationed to the right of you, the Frenchman to the left of you passes in front of you to get to the communal towel.

I suppose it wouldn't bother me if I were sure the man is really a Frenchman. What bothers me is that he may be a countryman of mine who has thrown away his Fielding's and is finding his own fun places.

By the way, I don't know if Fielding covers it, so I will. I mean that extra plumbing fixture you find in bathrooms on the Continent, the dynamics of which are most refreshing when explored in depth. That covers it.

If you're going to Italy and you haven't learned the language, you'll find there isn't too much of a language barrier. Italians gesture an awful lot and if you're facing them you can pretty much understand what they're trying to say.

In Rome, where there's all that pinching going on, even when your back is turned you can understand pretty much what a Roman is trying to say.

I've got to hand it to the Venetians though. I can't tell you how impressed I was with that city. Nowhere else in the world can you find a flood area bringing in so much tourist gold. Any other city in that condition would've been declared a disaster area and the Red Cross would've been in there evacuating the residents.

I don't care what the travel folders say, this city was not planned to be on water.

All you have to do is take one look at what's floating around in those canals and you can see that the original city fathers goofed. Luckily for them, somebody on their Chamber of Commerce got the bright idea of making a tourist attraction out of a big sewage problem.

They even capitalized on their pigeon problem. Wait'll you see St. Mark's Square in Venice.

I was talking to Sid Caesar about my trip to Italy and he told me about an experience he had when he was in Rome.

When he got there he was very anxious to visit all the famous and infamous historical sites that were part of the history of ancient Rome.

To overcome the language barrier, on the recommendation of the hotel manager, he engaged the very best guide in Rome.

The first place the guide took him was to the Pantheon. The guide started to tell Sid that this temple was built by Agrippa in 27 B.C. and was converted into a Christian church in 809 A.D. So Sid, who had been reading up on the sights he intended to see said, "You're 200 years off, it was converted into a Christian church in 609."

So the guide says to Sid, "You have the wrong information. I'm a Roman, so I must have the right information."

Sid didn't say anything until they got to the next historical site when the guide said, "This is the exact spot where Julius Caesar is buried."

"But nobody knows where Caesar is buried," said Sid.

"Romans know," said the guide, "and I'm a Roman."

Driving to the next stop the guide tells Sid that they are on their way to the palace of those two great Roman Emperors, Octavius and Augustus.

Again Sid corrected him saying, "Octavius and Augustus are one and the same. When Octavius became emperor, he was known as Emperor Augustus."

This inflamed the guide. To be corrected not once but three times and not even by a Roman but an American tourist was more than he cared to be corrected, so he turned to Sid and said, "How come you know so much, Mr. . . . Mr. . . ." Obviously searching for Sid's name.

"Caesar," said Sid.

"Caesar!" said the guide, "Well then, you should know!"

I'll never understand how some people "do the Louvre" in one morning.

I can't tell you how many mornings I have spent just in front of the Mona Lisa.

It's not that I'm such a big art lover. I'm in love with the art lovers who show up in front of her.

One morning I was standing in front of the Mona Lisa and this man standing next to me said to his wife, "For this you dragged me to Paris. We've got the same picture hanging in our bedroom."

And his wife said, "And in a nicer frame."

Another time a woman rushed past with her small daughter and said, "C'mon, walk! I'll tell you when we get to an important picture."

I heard one woman say to another, "I could die. I could just die. She's my sister-in-law's double."

I found language is no barrier for me in the Louvre.

I don't know if it was little Sam or little Serge or little Salvadore, or the language he was speaking, but I understood perfectly when his mother slapped him for pointing to a life-like manly statue and saying, "Look mama, papa!"

Ten

Who's Perfect?

I happen to be a great believer in putting off until tomorrow what I don't feel like doing today. I just don't have any self-discipline.

This doesn't bother me, but I have a neighbor who is a nut about self-discipline and it bothers her.

She dropped by one day and pointing to a big carton standing in the middle of the living room she said to me, "You've had that big carton standing in the middle of the living room for three weeks."

"Four," I said. "It came the week you were away visiting your mother."

"Aren't you going to open it?" she says.

"What for?" I said. "I know what's in it. Glasses."

So she says to me, "Then why don't you unpack them and put them away?"

So I said, "It's not that simple. I've got to find a place for them in the kitchen, and when I do unpack them all that stuff they pack glasses in will get all over the floor and I'll have to vacuum. I'll get around to it someday when I feel like it."

So she says, "Doesn't it bother you, standing like that in the middle of the room?"

So I said, "No. What bothers me is having to vacuum."

"If you take care of it," she says, "you have no idea how much better you'll feel."

"There's nothing wrong with the way I feel now," I said.

Then she says, "Well, I can't stand it. Would you mind if I did it?"

"Go right ahead," I said. "What I mind is having to do it myself."

Sure enough, she finds a place for the glasses, unpacks them, puts them away and vacuums the floor.

Then she says to me, "Why don't you give up smoking? I did."

"I did too," I said. "Several times."

"Just a little self-discipline goes a long way. You should try it, Selma," she says.

"I did," I said. "Several times."

Now she says to me, "I guess it has to be taught as a child. I was taught self-discipline as a child and I've practiced self-discipline all my life. I face every problem as it comes. My house is always in order and I do whatever has to be done no matter how I hate doing it."

Suddenly she looked at her wristwatch and starting for the door she took her departure saying, "I've got to go. Today is my group therapy day."

꩜ The Audrey Hepburn Caper

Have you ever seen that perfume advertisement around in magazines that's a big picture of Audrey Hepburn and underneath her picture it says "Once She Was the Only Woman in the World Allowed to Wear This Perfume."

What's more, this advertisement continues to announce that now: "Anybody Can Wear It."

Well, I would like to know what Miss Hepburn did that's so terrible that this great privilege was taken away from her. What was this great sin she committed to be publicly reprimanded?

Even worse than poor Hester Prynne.

Even Lizzie Borden was acquitted.

Doesn't this perfume company have any heart at all? Maybe I better take that back. Obviously the perfume company has some kind of heart because in spite of being a French company they did not sentence her to the guillotine.

When I first started seeing this advertisement around I was going to write to the company and ask them to tell me what she did that made them so mad. But I didn't. Supposing my letter got them mad at me.

They could alert the French Sureté that I was an international troublemaker and keep me out of Paris.

That stopped me.

But I can't stop thinking about what Miss Hepburn did that's so unforgivable.

Did she leave the stopper out of the bottle and the stuff evaporated before she used it all up? The French are quite penurious, you know.

Maybe it fell out of her hand and the bottle broke. Even that, what could it mean to the perfume company to send her another bottle? After all, they're getting it wholesale, even less than wholesale. Since they make the stuff they can afford to send it to her at cost.

Maybe her husband was allergic to it. It could happen. Now what kind of life is that? She's in her bed with the perfume and he's in bed with hives . . . so naturally she gave up the perfume. But surely a French perfume company should forgive Miss Hepburn for this. You know how they're supposed to be about bedding down, unless of course, it's just talk. . . . No, it couldn't be, it absolutely couldn't just be talk. I've been to Paris. Conversations are the least I think of when I think of Paris. London, yes. Paris, no.

What could it be? And how did the perfume company find out? Was somebody in her household, in the pay of the perfume company, watching what she did with their perfume . . . that's it.

I'll tell you one thing, I don't care that we're all allowed to buy that perfume. I'm not going to buy it. I'm not putting myself in any position where I'll be spied upon.

I don't always put on perfume when I'm fully dressed. Sometimes when I'm only half dressed. Most of the time when I'm not dressed at all. This could be the end of my privacy, not to mention my picture all over the place like Miss Hepburn's.

Cabbies Are My
Best Entertainment

When I tip a cab driver, I don't do it for the service I'm getting. I get the same service on a bus without tipping the driver.

I always think of it as an entertainment tax. You always get a lot of conversation from a cab driver which you don't get from a bus driver, unless of course you get on the bus with a five-dollar bill.

One morning I looked in my linen closet and I noticed all my towels were from hotels.

You know how it is when you're checking out of a hotel. You have a wet bathing suit, so you wrap your wet bathing suit in a dry hotel towel. Sometimes when you're checking out, you wrap a dry hotel towel in a dry hotel towel.

So I decided to buy towels. Because lately in first-class hotels I was getting second-class towels. I'm not lugging mended towels home. And there's no point in complaining to the management about the towels not worth taking home because that may be what they have in mind when they put those towels in my room.

I saw an advertisement in the paper that Macy's was having a sale on towels so I decided to go there.

I get in a cab and tell the driver to take me to Macy's.

As we're driving along, the cab driver is giving out with the biggest moaning and groaning.

I'm never alarmed at this because moaning and groaning are the occupational sounds cabbies make.

Once I asked a cabbie why he was moaning and groaning and he told me. What's more, I got so interested in his X-rays I went 80 cents out of my way.

This day, when I asked the cabbie why he was moaning and groaning he said, "This is it."

I said, "What?"

He said, "The world is coming to an end."

I said, "Before we get to Macy's?"

"Lady," he says, "don't you know what's going on?"

"I didn't know about this," I said. "I didn't read about it in the papers."

So he says to me, "Sure you didn't read about it in the papers. They don't tell you anything in the papers."

Then he says, "You'll read about it when it's over. Like now, the papers are full of space travel like it's something new."

"Take it from me, lady," he continued, "space travel is nothing new. It's been going on for years."

This surprised me, so I said, "Really?"

"Really," he says, "really. They're carrying on like there's nobody on the moon."

Now he starts talking about people living on the moon and he makes it sound like the A&P is up there.

Women are running to Orbach's up there. Howard Johnson's is up there with a new flavor, Moon Crater Crunch.

So I said to him, "Are you sure?"

"Of course, I'm sure," he said. "And I'll tell you something else. People from the moon are living *here*."

Now this I believe, because one of them is driving me to Macy's.

I don't like to antagonize somebody from another planet, so I said to him, "Don't worry about them blowing up the world. There's room for all of us."

Now he says, "For how long!? What about the population explosion?"

So I said, "What about it?"

Because as far as the population explosion, my conscience is clear.

"I'm for blowing up the world," he announces suddenly. "People are no good. I've been married for twenty-five years and my wife hates me!"

"I'm sorry," I said.

"Don't be sorry," he says. "I hate her too."

"How can you live like this?" I asked. "Why do you stay together?"

"Because it's easy," he says. "After twenty-five years . . . am I going to start hating a stranger?"

I was about to mention having a little faith . . . believing in kindness, but we were practically at Macy's and besides that'll be taken care of when he gets Billy Graham in his cab.

When I got out of the cab I tipped him most generously. If he was right and the world was coming to an end, why should I be stuck with a lot of cash?

I'm always in such a rush to get out of the house in the morning that I usually put my make-up on in the cab.

So as usual I'm in a cab on my way to work, gluing, stroking, blending and brushing. As I get out of the cab, the driver turns to me and says, "Lady, you looked good to me when you got into the cab before you put all that stuff on."

I tipped him big.

When I got to work I was telling the other writers

how this cab driver set me up in a good mood for the whole day.

Then Jay Burton who was writing on the Berle show with me told me about the time he was in a cab with Milton Berle.

Berle and the cab driver got to talking about baseball and before you knew it, they had made a bet on the outcome of that day's game.

As Berle gets out of the cab, he says to the driver, "You better let me have your address. In case I lose, I'll know where to send the check."

So the cab driver writes down his address and as Berle starts walking away, the driver says, "Wait a minute, mister, if you don't mind I'd like to have your name and address."

"I'm Milton Berle," says Berle.

The cab driver looks at him and says, "Am I supposed to recognize you? Do you know how many people are in and out of my cab all day?"

So Berle says, "I'm Milton Berle. I'm on television. Everybody watches me on television."

"Not me," says the cab driver.

Goodman Ace told me about the time he got into a cab and gave the driver his address and the driver said, "What did you say?"

So Goody repeats the address and the cabbie says, "I'm sorry, but I don't understand you."

By now Goody is a little miffed so he says, "Isn't this

murder? I was on radio for over twenty years making my living as an actor."

And the cab driver turned around and said to him, "And you know something—I didn't understand you then either!"

Once I got into a cab and just as I got settled the cabbie said to me, "Just my luck, night and day it's you. Night and day."

He's saying "night and day" but not in the mood that Cole Porter had in mind. Nor does it sound very much like the romance Fred Astaire gave it when he sang it to Ginger Rogers. Well, I can take a hint. So I said, "If I'm making you unhappy I'll be glad to take another cab."

So he said to me, "You're sitting. Then sit."

So I said, "What's this big problem I seem to be giving you?"

So he says, "You have no idea how many sleepless nights I've had on account of you and Johnny Carson."

Then he says to me, "I'm not a fan of yours and I can live without Johnny Carson too."

"Well then don't stay up watching the Tonight Show," I said. "Go to sleep."

"Go to sleep?" he asked. "I've tried it but it doesn't work. My wife is a big fan of the Tonight Show and every night she stays up and watches."

"Okay," I said. "What's the big deal? Let her watch and you go to sleep."

So he says to me, "It doesn't work that way. I go to sleep, she watches and when the show is over, she wakes me up to tell me what she saw."

Don't Call Me, I'll Call You

I used to keep the phone right near me all the time. The minute it rang I'd pick it up. In case it was Cary Grant.

I've given all that up. Cary Grant is never going to call me. Now I keep my phone in the closet and ignore it because that phone was driving me out of my mind. It was those wrong numbers.

The pattern is always the same. Somebody calls up, you tell them they've got a wrong number. You hang up and immediately they're on the phone again. They just can't believe they've got the wrong number and it takes at least two more calls to convince them.

Now if I'm working, right after that first wrong number I can't get back to work because I know the phone is going to ring again. I just sit there waiting for the second shoe to drop. Occasionally after the second shoe there's a third shoe.

It could be somebody from another planet dialing a wrong number. I don't care what advances have been made on earth and on other planets as regards exact sciences. Nobody anywhere has worked out an exact science for not dialing wrong numbers.

For a while there I couldn't sleep nights until I learned without a doubt that the hot line between Washington and the Kremlin was not a dial phone.

I did work out some means of dealing with wrong numbers which you're welcome to use if you're still waiting for Cary Grant to call you or Brigitte Bardot if you're of the other persuasion.

There was a girl who used to call my number by mistake and say, "Is Arnold there?"

The last time she called, instead of saying, "You've got the wrong number" and hanging up to wait for her to call again with, "Is Arnold there?" I said, "Yes, hold on, I'll get him."

I left my receiver off the hook and left her holding on. By the time I came back in an hour to replace my receiver she was no longer holding on. What's more I never heard from her again. This girl is so mad at Arnold for keeping her waiting that *he'll* never hear from her again either.

Nasty weather brings on a lot of wrong numbers. Especially from women who do their shopping by phone instead of going out. Whenever my phone rang for Gristedes, I said, "Yes" and took the order. I can't tell you what happiness I distributed to women calling the butcher and promising them lean bacon. All the fat cut off before weighing. And I promised soup bones and free parsley to everybody.

No matter how often you change your number to avoid all this nonsense it does you no good. Because the new number the phone company gives you is somebody's old number.

With all the services now available to the public by just dialing the phone, I found I was taking orders for Dial-A-Car or Dial-A-Pizza.

Whatever they were dialing for I gave them.

In New York, where I live, they also have a service from one of the local banks they call Dial-A-Loan. These wrong dialers I turned down.

On Sundays I'd get an awful lot of calls for Dial-A-Sermon. I always said a few words.

Once I got "Gloria's" old number. Night and day men were calling "Gloria." She must've offered some kind of service too. Probably Dial-A-Girl.

Then, of course, there are all those people with spare time who have been answering those advertisements "How To Make Money In Your Spare Time" by selling magazine subscriptions. My spare time is shot just getting them off my line.

Other calls that are taking up the time I could be dancing, are department store sales "specials."

It usually starts with Macy's calling up about the greatest stocking special since legs were invented. I don't care that the word around is that Macy's doesn't tell Gimbels. It's just not true. Because right after I hang up on Macy's, Gimbels calls up and offers me the very same bargain.

When I've had people over for dinner I expect the calls that come the next day from gracious guests who want to compliment me on the dinner and tell me what a fine time they had.

What I don't want are those calls that start off with, "Selma I don't know how to say this . . ." and then they go on to say, "Did anybody else who was there last night get food poisoning?" or "I checked with my garage and they assured me my tank was full when I pulled my car out. How well did you know the couple who arrived after me and were parked right next to me in your driveway?" or "Is my husband still there?"

Once I got a call that I'm really glad I didn't miss.

For days afterward I kept the phone out of the closet hoping something else as good would come along, but it didn't.

The call I'm talking about came from the mother of a girl I knew many years ago in the old neighborhood.

Her mother called me to invite me to the bridal shower being given for her daughter. I accepted. It would be nice to see these people again and just as I thought the conversation was coming to an end, the mother said to me, "I think you know the fellow my daughter is going to marry. He's also from our old neighborhood."

So I said, "Really, what's his name?"

Now she says, "He's such a nice fellow. Such nice

manners. I know his whole family and you must remember them too."

So I said, "What's his name?"

So she says, "He's no stranger to me. He's been coming into the house now for ten years. I know you know him."

So I said, "What's his name?"

Then she says, "Let me think for a minute."

I let her think.

Soon she gave up thinking and said to me, "I don't know his name but he owns his own business."

Being involved with TV I get quite a few calls from parents who can't be talked out of believing that their children are ready for stardom. So far I've been able to talk them out of it except for one instance.

This stage mother was more than a match for me. I did talk her out of bringing her small son up to my house to audition for me but I had to settle for his auditioning right then and there on the phone.

I held that receiver while this kid sang the whole score of "My Fair Lady." I applauded the kid's industry if not his talent and for an encore, to assure me that he was ready in case his voice changed prematurely, this kid sang the whole score from "The Man of La Mancha."

Those must be some bills that mother is running up with the telephone company.

That's why I wish there was something I could do for this kid's future, because *he's* doing a lot for my AT&T, which I'm depending on for my future.

Kids on the phone never make me too happy. They don't listen. They just talk. I have a friend who has a small girl of pre-school age and when I call my friend and the girl answers, I just hang up because it's always the same.

I call. The kid answers and says, "Hello." Now in the background I hear the mother saying, "Ask who it is."

The kid says, "Who is this?"

I say, "Miss Diamond."

But she isn't listening.

So isn't it better to hang up than to spend the next ten minutes while the mother in the background is yelling, "Ask who it is"?

The kid is yelling, "Who is this?"

And I'm yelling, "Miss Diamond."

Once kids have learned that part of talking on the phone is listening too, it is possible to have quite intelligent phone conversations with them.

I once worked with a writer on a television show who had a small daughter with whom I had a most stimulating conversation. I called his home one day.

She answered the phone and I said, "Hi pussycat, let me talk to your daddy."

And she said, "I can't."

I said, "Has he gone out?"

She said, "No."

So I said, "Well, then why can't you get him to the phone?"

And she said, "Because he's in Mummie's bed!"

It's Awful To See
A Man Cry

I thought that only women shoppers ran the gauntlet of trying to get waited on in exclusive Fifth Avenue shops.

I now find that Madison Avenue men's shops hold the same terror for men shoppers.

The more exclusive the shop, the higher standards the salespeople have set for their customers . . . or their clients as they refer to them.

I must explain that the owners of these shops have set up no such standards for their customers. With the rent sky-high and the overhead getting higher and higher, the only standard he has set for customers is . . . buy!

As a matter of fact, as far as the owners are concerned, you can come in and just look around. The owners still believe in catering to customers. He's the one who has to meet the bank's payments.

But what do the salespeople care if one of the biggest discount houses is doing a big clothing business in their branch on Fifth Avenue, which is only one block from Madison Avenue. They get paid every week.

However, it's the salesman who's around when you walk into a men's shop on Madison Avenue.

And he doesn't return your salute until he's close enough to read the emblem on your yachting cap.

If you're not wearing a yachting cap, it's not wise to paint the name of your yacht across your forehead.

Unfortunately a yacht owner I know didn't have his yachting cap and a hot-headed salesman seeing his painted forehead, threw him out. He assumed my friend was trying to pass as a yacht owner.

My friend never went shopping without his yachting cap again.

There is no point in trying to fake the name of a yacht. Because these salesmen are really with it.

They all know what B.B.D.&O. stands for. What's more, every morning they show up at B.B.D.&O. for the flag raising.

I was told an incident which involved a salesman who fell short of the Madison Avenue Corps.

A man came into the store wearing drip-dry shorts and fully knowing this, seeing the man without his pants in the fitting room, the salesman sold him a suit.

Selling a suit to a man who does his own undies is a treasonable act.

The salesman was immediately taken into custody and removed to Brooks Brothers to await his court martial.

And right there in Brooks Brothers' window, he was tried, found guilty and publicly stripped of his vicuna swatches.

It's awful to see a man cry.

Household Help Wanted

It seems to me that almost every woman I know is complaining about not being able to get competent household help these days.

I've gone through the same thing myself, so I know what they're talking about.

I've got a cleaning woman coming in now who is a whiz. The first day she came to work I could see she knew how to clean a house.

I'll never forget how impressed I was when she showed up exactly on time. In one hour she was ready to go to work after a leisurely breakfast which she cheerfully prepared for herself. I like a cheerful houseworker.

She stacked her breakfast dishes neatly in the dishwasher and suggested that I do the same after I had my breakfast. Why use up all that electricity to turn on the dishwasher just for her dishes when I could do mine and hers at the same time? I like an economical house-worker.

Then she went downstairs to the laundry room to wash and iron her uniform. An hour later she came upstairs spotless. I like a neat houseworker.

Then she said to me, "Are you still eating your breakfast? My, you're slow."

At last I had a houseworker who wasn't one for wasting my time.

In the living room she went to work cleaning up right away. She looked around and said to me, "Don't you ever pick anything up? It only takes a minute to empty ashtrays."

Then, pointing to the box the laundry comes in, she said to me, "That laundry should be taken out of the box and put away the minute it's delivered."

While she went down to the store to replace every mop, broom and cleaning aid I had with a mop, broom and cleaning aids that she could work with, I picked up everything that was lying around, emptied the ashtrays and put the laundry away.

I was so glad to have her. My place looked better already.

When she came back upstairs she didn't waste any time getting into her streetclothes and drank her hot beef broth standing up. Her time with me for that morning was up.

After she left I dusted and swept. I didn't want to do it in front of her. She might take it as criticism and never show up again.

But I must say this. When it came to the heavy cleaning she never let me down.

I had the painters in and I don't have to tell you what a mess that is.

If this houseworker hadn't shown up, I would still be living in that mess. Without her I wouldn't even have known where to start.

She showed up, bad back and all, and *told* me where to start. Bad back and all, she stayed a full day until I got everything in shape again.

When my neighbor asked me if my houseworker could give her a few mornings a week, I recommended her in the highest terms.

After all, it was from her that I learned how to do my housework.

Man Is Dog's Best Friend

I want to make it clear right away that I am not against dogs. As a matter of fact, I'm very fond of dogs. Some of my best friends have them. They and their dogs are always welcome in my home. With one exception. Both must be housebroken.

What's more, even though the pet-shop owner has put a sign in the window warning against the danger of leaning against the window, I have leaned dangerously to look at the puppies.

I lean there and go "Ahhhh. Ohhh. Oooo . . . Look at the one sleeping . . . oh . . . Look at the one scratching . . . oh . . . Look at the one fighting. I could take them all home."

So you can see I'm not against dogs. I have always had a dog and the only reason I don't have a dog now is because living in a city apartment I would be denying a dog his basic rights and freedoms. The right to run free and chase cats. The right to run free and chase dogs. The right to mate with those of his own choosing whenever and wherever. City dogs don't mate. They are bred. And even worse, castration without representation.

What's the sense of being a dog if you can't live like one!

To me, a dog is a dog. I think it's silly to think of him as a member of the family, because he doesn't.

You always read about somebody leaving money to their dog in their will.

Did you ever read about a wealthy dog leaving money to a person?

No sir! When a wealthy dog goes, he takes it with him.

When I see city people leading their dogs on a leash, I also see the dog is leading them by the nose.

Dog owners are out in all kinds of weather. They tell you it's small payment for the love their dogs bear them.

Some love. If that dog weren't on a leash he'd be off like a flash after another dog, a cat or any stranger walking along the street with a wet bag of meat.

If dog owners walked around in all kinds of weather for the postal service they'd really know love. A retirement plan. Social security. Medical insurance. Pension.

Did your dog ever send you a Valentine card?

I read of a woman who accused her husband in their separation hearing of putting a dog named Max Donovan on his payroll. This dog was on several mailing lists, paid income tax and belonged to a book club.

Do you think Max appreciated that this woman's husband raised him to this level of human friendship? He didn't because he's a dog. In trying to locate him they discovered he had headed for California leaving behind an unpaid bill with the Reader's Digest for $10.83.

I have an unmarried friend who has a dog for a constant companion. She's always urging me to get a dog to keep me company. Not me. When I think of a constant companion, I think of my dream prince—not somebody called "Prince."

A widowed lady I know insists that her loneliness would be unbearable without her dog.

I'll admit that you can warm your feet on the back of a poodle, but will a poodle get up in the middle of the night to get you a drink of water?

He's A Mess Without Make-up

I went into Bloomingdale's one day to buy some soap. As I'm picking out the soap, there's a woman standing next to me and she says, "You're buying the wrong soap."

I said, "What do you mean I'm buying the wrong soap?"

So she says, "Buy the soap I'm buying."

So I said, "Why should I do that? This is the soap I always buy."

Now she says to me, pointing to the soap she's buying, "My husband is crazy about this soap."

So I said to her, "Your husband isn't around when I'm taking a bath."

So she says to me, "I'll send him over."

She'll never send him over. . . . But we got to talking and I found out that the soap she's buying is not for herself but for her husband.

Then the salesgirl starts telling me that every day more and more men are stopping at her counter to buy soap for themselves. And then she points to a counter about two aisles away and tells me that on that counter I can find a complete line of cosmetics for men.

And that's exactly what I saw over there, cosmetics for men.

I look at this stuff and I see there's cosmetics for the face zone. Cosmetics for the body zone. They've got the American male cut up in more zones than divided Berlin.

I can understand this trend. Men have been faking it up to now in other areas so cosmetics for men had to happen.

Men wear toupees. The skinny ones wear falsies in their shoulders. Elevator shoes have been popular with men for years so that he can be taller than she is.

Well now, with cosmetics, he can not only be taller than she is, he can be prettier.

Who knows, the next time you're sitting in the Play-boy Club, your bunny may be Gerald.

Although I don't think topless waiters will create too much excitement.

I have a cute dentist . . . and who knows, with cosmetics and all, he may turn up soon as Playmate of the Month.

When you stop and think about it . . . in the jungle the male animal is the more colorful, and especially male birds.

I don't mind men identifying with jungle animals. I like it. It's the men who identify with birds that worry me. I hate to think of them wanting to fly a little.

𝕩 Cocktails At Four

I'm giving up going to those big noisy cocktail parties people give around the winter holidays.

You know the kind. The hostess is getting rid of all her year-round social obligations with this one big happening.

When I've had somebody over for a sit-down dinner, I don't need to be paid off in onion-soup dip.

I never arrive at a cocktail party so hungry that I have to start eating right away. But it seems to me everybody else there did. By the time I do feel like having something, all that's left at the buffet is a couple of colored-plastic cocktail picks floating around in the watery shrimp bowl. And part of a meatball slowly moving down the side of the chafing dish. That's why the onion-soup dip is still there.

And I don't need those frozen canapes they're heating in the kitchen to take care of party crashers.

As the party progresses you can see everybody getting blind. That's when the hostess starts putting it away pretty good too because she can see what's happening to her rug.

Usually, to give the party class, there's a hired piano player.

It doesn't matter how good he is because you can't hear with all the noise going on. But it does take care of the girls who came to the party unescorted and will go home that way. They hang around the piano requesting songs from "Lady in the Dark," "Brigadoon" and "Having a Wonderful Time."

The piano player knows all these songs because he's been playing at cocktail parties as long as the girls have been coming to them unescorted.

Fellows who come without a date and are going to leave that way join this group. Every fellow isn't a prize, either.

Another thing that I can do without is being greeted by the hostess with, "Come along with me. There's somebody here who is sooooooo anxious to meet you."

Just as she starts leading me to this "somebody who's so anxious to meet me," some more people arrive. She leaves me standing in the middle of the room while she goes off to greet them with the same brazen-faced lie.

I always look around for somebody who looks anxious to me. So far the only anxious face I see coming toward me is the hired help trying to unload a tray of something very limp, lying across something very soggy.

Knowing that this kind of happiness is all I ever find at these parties, you'd think I'd have given up going to them a long time ago. It's the come-on that gets me every time.

Just as I'm about to turn down an invitation, the party-giver says, "Oh you must come. Sinatra is in town and he promised to drop by."

I happen to be a big Sinatra fan. So I go. The only trouble is that no matter when I get to the cocktail party, Sinatra just left.

Late or early, Sinatra just left!

I once showed up at a cocktail party so early, the hostess was still running around in her slip, the host was taking the kids over to his mother's to get them out of the way and as I walked in the hostess said to me, "Sinatra just left."

Once I stuck around until there was nobody left at the party but me and the handyman from downstairs who was breaking down the bathroom door because one of the guests forgot his date was in there and left with another girl.

Since the hostess was back in her slip and the host was over at his mother's picking up the kids, I was the only one around in condition to take the hysterical, rejected female downstairs and put her in a cab.

And while I was downstairs trying to help the poor creature fix a flat rate with the cab driver to her analyst in Newark, I heard later, "Sinatra came and left."

Eleven

Escaping Into Realism

There's a thing going on in movies today that I don't understand at all. The anti-hero gets the girl.

What am I talking about, "gets the girl" . . . he gets *all* the girls.

You've seen those pictures where the male star goes from girl to girl to girl to girl. One is never enough for him.

Now what is this? I remember when Lana Turner was not only enough for Clark Gable, but there was plenty left over for every man in the audience.

And how about the trend in romantic pictures where there is just *one* girl to a fellow?

To make it real, the audience must understand the motivation that brings the boy and girl together. So all throughout the picture these two out-patients sit around probing each other's psyche. It's no longer a love story unfolding on the screen. It's a case history.

I don't have to remind you that when Lana Turner was the sweater girl, right away the audience understood Clark Gable's motivation.

And what happened to the hero and the heroine's "cute" meeting?

You knew if the opening scene was in a cafeteria and Betty Grable accidentally spilled noodle soup over a fellow's head, the fellow under those noodles was Dan Dailey.

You also knew that they were destined to become the top Mr. and Mrs. dancing team on Broadway, and you were happy for them.

And when Paulette Goddard, perfectly tattered by Edith Head, fought the other beggars for the coins flung from the royal carriage, you knew that in spite of Vincent Price and Basil Rathbone, she would end up riding in that royal carriage.

And in the pictures they used to make, unmarried good girls did not have babies. Unless of course it was one in which John Boles was the father which was okay because John Boles always came back sometime after World War I to marry the girl.

There's a new kind of romance on the screen that has come to us from Sweden. It can be boy meets boy. Girl meets girl. Undecided meets undecided. Or any combination thereof.

While this kind of romantic picture may seem odd to us, you must remember that over there the sauna bath is a way of life.

The husband and wife films made in this country today throw me.

I remember Mrs. Miniver was a nice lady. Mrs. Chips an angel. Even Mrs. Skeffington, who was so rotten to Claude Rains in the beginning of the picture made up for it in the end.

Mrs. Miniver never opened a big mouth like Elizabeth Taylor in "Who's Afraid of Virginia Woolf?"

I never saw Mrs. Miniver hitting the bottle either.

Maybe once in a while she'd take a little wine with her dinner, but you never saw Mrs. Miniver smashed.

In all those pictures where Bette Davis was married to George Brent, even though she was the kind who went looking for extramarital action, it was never in front of George Brent. She always shot him to save him embarrassment. She was an example of wifely respect.

Not Elizabeth Taylor in "Who's Afraid of Virginia Woolf?" Not only did she carry on in front of her husband with a man who was a lot younger, but who was also a lot thinner.

All those Andy Hardy pictures will probably be preserved as museum pieces. Those popular "man-to-man talks" between Andy and his father, Judge Hardy, will remain a quaint reminder of our primitive past when a teenager could communicate with an "over-thirty."

I hope Disney doesn't take to making films that analyze in depth.

I'll be destroyed if it ever turns out that Prince Charming wasn't looking for Cinderella at all. And that he was running around with her slipper because he was queer for feet.

Waddya Read?

Have you noticed that women's magazines are divided into two groups.

Besides what they cost and the slickness of the paper on which they are printed, they are mostly distinguishable by the picture of the girl on the cover.

One group usually shows a girl, young, fresh, not an emerald in sight, with a warm friendly smile for the whole world. You know, the "girl-next-door."

Now the girl on the covers of the other group has obviously been more choosy about whom she's smiling at because she's covered with emeralds and has moved out of your neighborhood.

Inside the first group of magazines you'll find pictures of fifty-year-old women who are proud to be fifty.

Inside the second group you find pictures of fifty-year-old women who wouldn't admit to being fifty if they live to be a hundred.

And of course, the approach to sex is quite different.

The first group seems to take a clinical approach . . . like "Conversations With Your Family Doctor" . . . and from these conversations, this first group seems to have just discovered sex.

While in the second group, they seem to have dispensed with the middle man, did their own field work and were the ones to discover sex in the first place.

And there's quite a difference in meal planning too.

In the first group of magazines they show you how to feed sixty people at a sit-down church supper with a No. 2 size can of tuna fish and three potato chips. What's more, this recipe is followed with a few hints of how to stretch the leftovers with a sprig of parsley for the next sit-down church supper.

Naturally the second group of magazines has no suggestions for leftovers. Their plan for a sit-down church supper is to jet your sixty guests to Vatican City and have all the food flown in from Maxim's in Paris.

And another thing, it seems that everybody who reads the first group has a trunk up in the attic that is a bottomless pit of heirloom lace. They show you how to make your daughter's first formal out of your wedding gown, which your mother made out of her mother's bedspread, which she made out of her mother's antimacassars, which her mother made from the lace shirt which the Hessian mercenary left behind when he just grabbed his pants and jumped out of the window. Of course, they don't mention how they came into the possession of this lace shirt, but let's face it, even the Colonial Army must have warned our women against fraternizing with the enemy.

Now in the second group of magazines, the ancestors of their readers never touched his shirt. Instead, they gave him the run of the house and a false sense of security so that he never removed his money when he removed his pants.

So *they* removed his money, invested it wisely and today have a trunk up in the attic that is a bottomless pit of money. . . . Waddya read?

Smile, You're On Picture Phone

AT&T has announced that the picture phone will soon be a reality. With the picture phone, both the telephoner and the telephonee will be able to see as well as hear each other.

When I first read about this, I got pretty excited.

When I started to think about it, I calmed down.

Just as you're beginning to enjoy some new thing, a wise guy comes along with something newer and spoils it all.

Like when fire was first discovered. For centuries we enjoyed the pleasure of cooked foods. So what happened, along came TV dinners and that was the end of that pleasure.

Then somebody came up with steam heat and just as we're all sitting around warm and cozy in our apartments, landlords came along and discovered turning it off.

I don't have to tell you what happened when Freud discovered sex.

However, I must admit that this picture phone is going to be a big time saver.

Up until now, when a fellow called a girl to make a blind date, they had to spend a whole evening together to be disappointed in each other.

With the picture phone there will be the advantage of instant disappointment! Just call up! Take a look! Hang up!

Husbands who call their wives to say they're working late, will have to be very careful that the picture phone doesn't pick up the drink they're holding. Not to mention the doll they just picked up.

If you happen to be the Playmate of the Month, I wouldn't pass the word around that your phone always rings when you're in the shower and you have to run out soaking wet to answer it . . . because all kinds of people will be calling you with offers to make you their playmate of the day.

Naturally, with the picture phone, the FCC will move in and it's a good thing, too. When the other party on your line ties it up for hours and you're stuck every time you want to use your phone, with the FCC in there, you'll be able to demand equal time so that you can tie up the party line.

I can't wait to get my picture phone because it's the surest way I'll ever be able to cut down on my bills.

During the winter I'm going to put my phone calls on video tape. During the summer I won't have to use my phone at all. I'll just watch the reruns.

Whatever Happened To Baby Dolls?

I went into a toy store to buy a doll for a small girl and I discovered something. There's no such thing as a doll anymore. What they're selling in toy stores for small girls these days aren't dolls.

This hit me when I asked to see a doll and the clerk

showed me one wearing horn-rimmed glasses. A myopic doll!

I asked what this thing cost and she told me. So I said to her, "For this money I'd like to see a doll with 20/20 vision."

She brings out another one. A talking doll this time. And she explains to me that this talking doll has a vocabulary of over 140 words.

As far as I'm concerned, this is more than a talking doll. This is a doll with a big mouth.

Think of it, a vocabulary of over 140 words. This doll is a Bennington graduate.

How can I give a doll like this to a kid who is a problem reader? Her mother would kill me. There's nothing in Dr. Spock that covers sibling rivalry between a kid and a talking doll.

I always thought that the reason little girls play with dolls was somehow tied up with the mother instinct. Now what little girl is going to enjoy mothering a doll who talks back?

When I was a small girl, my mother painted a face on a clothespin and I was emotional about that clothespin for years. That clothespin really needed me. Believe me, there is nothing more helpless than a clothespin.

What fun is a self-sufficient doll?

And these dolls the clerk was showing me were pretty well dressed. The wardrobe available for them ranged as high as five hundred dollars. Standing next to these dolls I felt shabby. I even looked shabby.

Then she showed me a teenage boy doll that was perfect for the teenage girl doll. Up until now I didn't know that dolls were going steady.

The way this looks to me is that the teenage problem has just become too much for adults and they're dumping it into the hands of the nursery crowd to see how they cope with it.

What game can a small girl play with boy and girl teenage dolls who want to neck?

Obviously these dolls are not brother and sister so she can't play house and be their mother. So what we have now is a six-year-old mother-in-law. That's a nice trauma to present to a little girl.

And you certainly can't push teenage dolls around in a doll carriage. There isn't a teenage boy doll in the world who hasn't got his eye on a sports car.

I can't see any fun for a small girl in this setup.

Can you see what this will do to her poor little ego as the dolls make it quite clear to her that two's company and three's a crowd.

How is she going to feel when she is put to bed at eight and her dolls can stay up to watch "The Late Show?"

This could start any normal little girl bed-wetting again.

Plants Are Only Human

It isn't enough to have a green thumb. If you want your plants to really knock themselves out for you, show them you have a green heart.

They've been doing some research with plants lately and they've discovered that plants respond to human companionship.

It's like the thing they did with cows and discovered that cows that have music playing while they're being milked give more milk. Not more cream, just more milk. What happens about more or less cream in milk has nothing to do with cows. Once it leaves them, it's between the farmer and his conscience.

Anyway, a couple of researchers took two house plants, put each one in the same planting medium, fed them the same plant food and placed them in the same atmospheric surroundings. However, one plant was given human companionship while the other remained attended to only by Mother Nature.

Both plants thrived, but the one that was given music to grow by and a word of encouragement as it grew outgrew and outblossomed the other one. This proved that plants react to a kind word . . . and what's more, a kind word does more for plants than fertilizer.

I think it's only fair at this point to make it clear that this is no attempt to knock Mother Nature. Considering the number of plants she's got to take care of she's been going pretty good. And let's not forget the added pressures put upon her by the modern world. She stands alone against "the pill." Even the church, which was always a dependable ally, is beginning to play footsies with the opposition. So it's quite understandable if the tomatoes you've been buying at the supermarket taste a little insecure.

Another thing they found out in experimenting with houseplants is that they react to tension. Can you imagine that? A petunia can get an ulcer!

This explains why you always see artificial plants in offices on Madison Avenue. Apparently live plants don't last any longer than account executives.

Talking to plants is not a new thing with me. I always talk to my plants when I water them. But I must say I didn't know they listened.

Now that I'm backed up by scientific research, I'm very careful what I say. Who knows, they may start talking back.

I've been watching my plants very carefully and I've noticed something about them that I never noticed before. You know how plants on the window sill always turn to face the sun. Well, on Sundays my plants turn and face "Meet the Press."

Now that I know they're interested in what's going

on, when I go out I leave the television set on so they won't miss Huntley and Brinkley.

And I don't worry anymore about who's going to water them when I'm out of town. With the set on, they can watch "Love of Life" and water each other.

I've been doing everything to close the communication gap between me and my plants. There was a time that whenever I'd have people over I'd always move my plants into another room. You know how stuffy it gets in a room with a bunch of people and most of them smoking. I found that if I left my plants in the room . . . they'd wilt.

Now I know they weren't wilting from the smoke. What was getting them down was being left out of the party.

My plants come to all my parties now. Before my guests arrive, when I water my plants I drop a little gin in the water. You have no idea how perky they stay all evening. But you've got to be careful they don't get hooked on the stuff. Philodendron don't even show it. A tipsy geranium is fun. A drunken begonia is bad enough but there's nothing more disgusting than a pussy willow with a snootful. Poinsettias really turn on.

New Year's Eve I had some people over and I let my plants toast the New Year.

After my guests left, I went to bed but my plants must've continued the party because the following Christmas there were petunias growing on my poinsettia plant.

I can't blame anybody but myself for this. You see,

my mother told me about people. She never mentioned a word about the bees and flowers.

This year I'm making sure my plants are protected against themselves. I got a house bee.

❦ The Return To The Ice Age

I've been giving considerable thought to this new medical discovery that involves freezing people. Medical science, right along with the Jolly Green Giant, has been experimenting with the process of deep freezing.

What the Jolly Green Giant has accomplished with tender young peas can now be accomplished with you.

They've discovered that when you're put in the deep freeze, no matter how long you're in there, you don't get any older. It doesn't matter if it's months or years. When you're defrosted, you're still garden fresh.

I don't have to tell you what a battle it is for a woman to stay young. This freezing process won't put an end to active combat but it certainly promises to reduce the fighting to what you might call a cold war.

Can you imagine with what enthusiasm this will be received by womankind?

Up until now there was absolutely no guaranteed method to stay at your best age unless you were one of Morton's Frozen Fruit Pies or an African lobster tail.

Naturally, beauty parlors, as we know them today, will be out. It's just a question of time until we read about the merger between Max Factor and Bird's-Eye.

And if you see a woman whose youthful appearance never changes, it won't be a question of, "Does she . . . or doesn't she?" Instead, you can be sure it's Westinghouse.

On the other hand if you see a woman who seems to be showing her age, the electrical outlets in her house are overloaded and her deep freeze is constantly breaking down. It could also be her rotten husband who keeps pulling the plug out.

Ladies, for heaven's sake, don't forget to pay your electric bill!

What's so great about this discovery is that you can have all the advantages of being Dorian Grey without cluttering up your attic with scary pictures.

And if you've got something for which there is no known cure now, you have yourself put on ice and labeled to be opened when somebody does come up with a cure.

Since this may take quite some time you'll be running up an awfully big electric bill, so forget this prospect of immortality unless you're loaded.

The way I see it, the only people who can afford immortality are the bunch with a corporate tax structure. The rest of us don't have enough left over after taxes to go on living to enjoy Medicare.

However, if you suddenly do come into money it might be smart to get yourself a little ice house in some low-rent district and hole up. You won't be paying any taxes if you're out of circulation.

And you not only will have frozen assets, you'll be one. This may not sound like such a good idea now but who knows, by the time the ice melts, money may be back in style.

Nudism Isn't Nakid
And Other Nakid Facts

It seems that every year more and more Americans are flocking to nudist camps. Now let me explain what nudists are.

You know the condition you're in when you're about to take a bath and suddenly there's no water because somebody is in the cellar fixing the pipes. Well, nudists are people running around in this same condition, but without the plumbing problem.

And if you're under the impression that nudist camps are filled with a bunch of sex-mad men and women up for grabs, forget it. The closest thing to Dionysian revelry with nudists is a game of volleyball.

How lusty can you get on Tiger's Milk and organic sunflower seeds?

They say that they see no more in each other than they see in the trees, the sun and the sky. Nudists say they are one with nature. I say nudists are a bunch of people with faulty vision.

In Sweden, where nudism is a general practice, the suicide rate is alarmingly high. Nudism may be a contributing factor.

It's not unlikely that a potential suicide gets very depressed comparing himself with some of the others.

On the other hand, I'd expect nudists to be a happy group. There are some people I know who would be good for a laugh if you saw them with their clothes off. I'm sure I'd get a chuckle.

In our puritanical country, we modestly lower our eyes in the sight of another's nakedness. But we do peek.

I don't remember if it was *Time* or *Newsweek* but in one of those magazines I read a story about how it has been statistically proven that a woman's brain is in direct relationship to the size bra she wears. In other words, in women, nature compensates for the underdevelopment of the brain by the overdevelopment of her development.

My first reaction to the story was that Hugh Hefner

had bought *Newsweek* and this story was part of the new editorial policy.

When I noticed that the middle fold picture was of Vice President Agnew, fully clothed, I knew the magazine had not changed hands.

I read that you no longer have to fuss with a series of aptitude tests to arrive at a woman's IQ.

You just put a tape measure around her and get her IQ that way. You may also get a punch in the nose but scientific research has many perils.

But what has all this fun and frolic in the scientific laboratory really contributed?

So flat-chested women know all the answers! What man wouldn't rather be with somebody in Sophia Loren's size bracket while both of you wrestle with the question?

If there is something to this theory, brainy women who have been eating a lot of dinners alone can now falsify their IQ in any lingerie department and never have to eat alone again.

Most discoveries, I've heard, are really mistakes made in research laboratories. That's what must have happened here. Some researcher married a girl who to all outward appearances was a luscious C cup "dumb-dumb" and on his wedding night discovered that she was really an A cup "Magna Cum Laude."

Where Babies And
Money Come From

I don't think there's anything wrong in an early sex education for young children. I just don't agree with the child psychologists who warn of irreparable harm in the sexual development of those children who are told that babies are brought by the doctor in his little black bag.

It so happens that I was one of those children who was told that the doctor brought me in his little black bag. It didn't do me any irreparable harm.

I think I was about thirty when I happened to look inside a doctor's bag and saw there were no babies in it.

You know what doctors have in those bags! Traffic tickets for illegal parking, argyle socks made by a grateful gall bladder patient, lots of angry literature from the American Medical Association against socialized medicine and a white shirt in case the doctor can make the theater. With all that stuff in there it would be impossible to carry a baby around too.

I didn't flip. Although the doctor whose bag I had

just examined went kind of nutty when I told him what I just found out. I never saw anything like it. Instead of pouring me a drink and showing me his new stereo equipment, which is why he happened to invite me up to his apartment in the first place, he just took me downstairs and put me in a cab. I never heard from him again.

As for me I felt fine. I just reconstructed my thinking.

I went back and saw some foreign art films that I had viewed purely as art the first time I saw them.

Now I saw them for what they are. I subscribed to *Cosmopolitan,* which I had heard, each month, vividly delineates modern woman's sexual role.

After two issues I canceled my subscription. I wasn't ready. I could see that Helen Gurley Brown's editorial guidance was for more advanced readers. To catch up to them I had considerable remedial reading to do. I'm doing great. The reading is fun and I'm planning a few field trips to augment the reading.

I honestly can't see where telling me that babies are brought by the doctor in his little black bag has caused me any irreparable harm.

The story I was told as a child that really has thrown my psyche is the one that begins, "Money is not Important."

What a thing to tell a small child. Money is very important. Money is a many splendored thing. How could Santa Claus bring all those toys if Papa didn't send him the money!

Anybody can be a Boy Scout but you need money to buy the official uniform.

Money has more uses than scotch tape. Compared to the power in money, the power in new liquid Ajax is a pussycat.

If I had known this when I was a small girl I could've put some away to use now that I'm a big girl instead of having to start looking around for it now.

Some of the methods for a big girl to acquire money are very interesting. One method is to marry a rich man. Another method is to divorce a rich man.

A combination of these methods has worked most successfully for the Gabors.

But I can forget about that because I don't have to tell you how they have eliminated all possible competition by combining their individual resources until you might say they have monopolistic control.

I am now looking into possible shady methods of acquiring money.

Most of them involve marriage. A wife has often accumulated quite a bundle jacking up her demands for more household money. For example, pushing tuna-fish casseroles at least twice a week under the guise of chicken and pocket the difference in the cost between tuna fish and chicken. This works quite well except that I have a friend whose husband is going out of his mind trying to figure out why he has suddenly begun to break out in a rash from chicken when all his life it was canned tuna to which he was allergic.

And he's never going to figure it out because only another chicken could tell it wasn't chicken in that casserole under all that undiluted Campbell's mushroom soup and crushed potato chips.

I'm going to rob a bank.

When I first got this idea there were many obstacles in my way.

It's inconvenient for me to rob a bank during the day because I'm working.

After work I'm too tired.

By the time I get home, shower, put on my bathrobe and have dinner on a tray, I don't feel like going out again to rob a bank.

And I'm not going to cancel a dinner date for that.

Sometimes I just forget.

Another obstacle is that camera set up around the bank that takes your picture.

Well, in front of the camera I can't use my street make-up. I'd have to get a professional make-up artist. I'm not spending fifty dollars to be made up just to rob a bank.

But I've got it all worked out now. I bank by mail. Next week when I send my deposit, in the space on the deposit slip where I usually put down the amount of my deposit, I'm going to write: THIS IS A HOLDUP!

Why My Interior Isn't Decorated

When Ladybird moved into the White House and started beautifying, it's exactly what any mother of marriageable daughters does.

Most mothers with marriageable daughters always start beautifying the house to impress their daughters' most desirable prospects when they come around to call for them.

Mr. Nugent and Mr. Robb must be a couple of real prizes because to impress them, Mrs. Johnson went around beautifying the whole country.

I got caught up in all this and I thought I'd do a little beautifying around my house. I'm still up for grabs. . . .

At the time I thought of this I was involved with a weekly television show and I didn't have the time to go chasing around the stores looking for things. So I decided I'd get a decorator and let her go chasing around.

In asking around, I got the name of a decorator from

a friend of mine and I called the decorator and made an appointment with her to come over.

The day she came over, she walked in, looked around, took out a little notebook and pencil and a carpenter's tape measure and started measuring and putting things down in her notebook.

Not a word came out of her for about ten minutes and then she said, "This is very exciting. There is so much I can do with your place. I want to get started right away."

And then she said, "Where will you be living?"

So I said, "What do you mean, where will I be living?"

So she says, "Well, you want to get rid of all the things in here now and until I get all your new things in, you'll have to find a place to live."

When I heard this, I just looked at this woman who until ten minutes ago was a complete stranger to me . . . and this stranger has walked into my house, declared it a disaster area and suddenly I'm being evacuated. I'm not happy about this at all.

She continues with her notebook and carpenter's tape measure. She's looking in my closets, shaking all the empty boxes I keep piled up in there and just leaves them on the floor after knocking them over herself.

"When I finish with this apartment," she says, "it will really fit your personality."

So I said, "How much is this going to cost?"

I figure, right away, I'll give her a clue to my personality.

She doesn't answer. She's climbing up on the window sills. The dust on the venetian blinds doesn't bother her . . . nothing bothers her, not even me.

"A woman," she says, "must have the right background. In the right background a woman unfolds like a flower."

Well, I'm not unfolding until I find out how much this is going to cost.

"How much is it going to cost?" I said.

So she tells me. I said, "Forget it. Leave the house the way it is and I'll keep my petals closed."

So she says to me, "That's where your thinking is wrong."

She says, "If you had this apartment set up right, you wouldn't want to keep changing it all the time. It will be a perfect background for you. All the things that I'll put in here will be things that you're going to like."

"What's more," she says, "you'll find that in your new surroundings, the more you live in it, the more you'll become attached to it. You'll love it."

I'll never love it! Who wants to get emotionally involved with furniture?

What! I'm going to put in my diary . . . "Today I discovered I love my bed. I think my bed is beginning to notice me."

It'll never happen. All my life I've been indifferent to furniture. I'm not going to change.

I've had a dinette set for ten years. Believe me, I have never exchanged two words with that dinette table or even one of the chairs.

I talk to my typewriter, but that's different, we work together and we have a business relationship. But that's all. After business hours my typewriter and I have nothing in common.

Once in a while I make a few rude remarks to my television set, when it's on. But everybody does. I can hardly consider those rude remarks a lovers' quarrel.

So with this in mind I said to the decorator, "I am not throwing everything out. Just give me a new look."

So she thinks for a while and she says, "I can do it. We can get some amusing antiques."

Now I know all about "amusing" antiques. I have a friend who has them all through her home. She puts ivy in those warming pans that they used to stick in the bed and she's got ivy in those things they used to stick under the bed.

I don't want my house cluttered up with this primitive plumbing.

Then I think . . . this woman is a decorator, maybe she knows and I don't know. So I said, "Go ahead."

The very next day she calls me and says, "I have found the perfect sofa for you. I want you to meet me and see it."

So I meet her in this antique shop on Third Avenue and I look at this sofa with the scratches all over the frame and the stuffing coming out of the seat cushions.

She says to me, "You've got to buy it."

I said, "What for? The one I've got in the house right now looks like this."

So she starts telling me what a real antique this sofa is and she shows me the worm holes in the wood, which is what makes owning it status.

I said, "How much is it?"

So she told me. That's when I gave up the whole idea of redecorating. And if worm holes are status, why spend all that money? If I were really interested, I'd just find a hungry worm and give it a good home.

Twelve

Nose Jobs
For World Peace

I have the secret for world peace. And you know what it is? Nose jobs! That's right, nose jobs for the whole world.

Think about it. I have. Look around you! You'll see that once somebody has their nose fixed, they never get into a fight.

What's more, they'll do anything, but anything to avoid a punch in the nose.

It's not like when you had your old nose. Your old nose didn't cost you anything so you don't care. Once you've had your nose fixed, you're for peace talks. New noses do not stand up in combat.

Once the people in all countries start having their noses fixed, the economy in all countries will really zoom. Plastic surgery is not cheap.

And I'll tell you another thing. Once you have your nose fixed, you'll want to have your teeth capped to go with your nice new nose.

This will bring about peace profiteering to enrich the whole world.

Just having your front teeth capped costs as much as a missile. Having your whole mouth capped can run into the price of an atomic submarine.

War plants will convert to dental laboratories. Employment will be at a new high. Dental technicians will all be wearing silk shirts and driving new cars.

The whole world will be smiling. It will have to be the end of wars forever.

Capped teeth don't stand up in combat either.

And the Nobel Peace Prize would go to the scientist who discovered a cure for baldness.

Diplomats Are Man Made

More and more women are being appointed to important diplomatic posts. I think it's great.

Now, if a woman dreams she met Kosygin in her Maidenform bra, it's not a dream. It's happening.

Recognition of women's potential in government should do more for shaping the image of the modern female than Lycra.

I was having dinner with a man on the very same day of another Presidential appointment going to a woman.

My date brought the subject up.

"Women," he said, "will never make good diplomats because by nature they're too single-minded to compromise."

I didn't tell him that the only reason I was having dinner with *him* was because I was tired of waiting for Gregory Peck to invite me to dinner.

"Women are too emotional," he continued. "A man always knows what a woman is thinking."

This one doesn't know that when he's kissing me good night I'm thinking of Gregory Peck.

"As for keeping secret information," he said, "anything a woman knows, the whole world is going to know."

I have never told this fellow how old I am or how much I weigh. He thinks I'm a natural blonde.

"It's a laugh," he laughed. "Women negotiating on an upper level. Women are not listeners."

So far all I was doing was listening.

Then he says to me, "All these appointments are just a political move to ensure women's votes."

It so happens that I know women don't vote in a bloc. I once went to a party and walked smack into another guest wearing an identical dress. Do you think we congratulated each other on having the same winner? No sir! We split the party.

❧ Select Craters
Now Available

Now that one race to the moon has been won and we landed the first man on the moon, there's another race to the moon coming up which should be equally exciting to watch.

The race to the moon between Howard Johnson and Hilton.

With each trip our astronauts will be spending more time there. As the length of their explorations on the moon is extended, they will eventually be looking around up there for living quarters.

I don't have to tell you what business it will mean for either Howard Johnson or Hilton to be able to be the first to advertise the opening of "THE ASTRONAUTS' EARTH AWAY FROM EARTH."

Whichever lucky enterprise it is, they will undoubtedly engage a bilingual staff, speaking both English and Russian.

Patriotism is one thing. Business is another.

Once it's established that people can live on the moon, here come the home-development companies.

They'll be up there next. They'll grab all those dust craters real cheap, fill them in and offer home-buying earthlings the nearest thing to heaven.

With the added attraction of your own private launching pad and easy financing, those homes will go like hot meteors.

Before you know it, there will be schools up there and the PTA will be on the moon.

With school drop-outs to follow, chasing around in souped-up space ships, swiping nose cones.

There will be a big problem getting a sleep-in maid

to go to the moon, because right now on earth it's getting pretty tough to get one to go to New Rochelle.

Getting a daily cleaning woman will also be a problem, unless of course you're willing to pick her up in the morning and return her in space in the evening so she can rendezvous with her bus.

It'll cost you a fortune in fuel living on the moon if your job is back here and you have to commute. But you've got to expect that living in the suburbs. At least you got your children off the crowded earth to where they can not only breathe fresh air but get right up and float around in it.

I hate to think of it but with all the traffic going on between the earth and the moon, before you know it, all that beautiful scenery along the outer spaceway will be ruined by dumps of abandoned, outdated relics of 1970 space ships.

And when the dust from those hastily filled-in craters starts seeping in and flooding the cellars of home owners, it'll really be a mess up there.

I just hope that NASA is looking far enough ahead in their planning to include an urban-renewal program.

❧ The Lack of Space Age

The apartment houses in New York are getting taller and taller. And the rooms are getting smaller and smaller. The closets are disappearing altogether.

When I go looking for an apartment, the first thing I look for is closet space. When I looked at the apartment I'm living in now, I got so excited when I saw the walk-in closet, I took it on the spot.

When I moved in, it turned out that what I thought was the walk-in closet was the bedroom.

There is a closet in the bedroom, but once the bed is in, you can't get to that closet unless you're a tinker toy. So I decided to use it to store things I'm not using. But my apartment is furnished with the things I'm not using because I can't give them away.

The Salvation Army turned down my black-and-white television set because they're stocked full. I know it would be a waste of time to offer it to Goodwill Industries because it's in good working condition, so it's no challenge for their workers.

Nobody wants to take my Magnavox unless I also

give them a one-year-service policy. As for the piano, you can't give a piano away unless Leonard Bernstein is at the keyboard.

I've tried everything to make more storage space. The first things to go were graduation pictures and diplomas. If anybody wants to know if I can read and write, they'll just have to take my word for it. Other pictures went too. Anytime I want to see what I looked like when I was a baby, I go down to the public library and look at a picture of Winston Churchill.

Somehow, in trying to fit into this lack-of-space age we're living in, you lose your identity.

You need that picture of your mother drying you off in the sand with that Brighton Beach Bath towel. And you need those sugar cubes, strung on pink ribbon and hanging from the ceiling at your "sweet sixteen" birthday party to prove you're alive.

You have no idea how many times I have jumped out of bed in the middle of the night to see if I cast a shadow.

I'm always calling the FBI to make sure they haven't lost my finger prints.

What gets me are those suggestions you see in slick, home-decorating magazines on how to use space you didn't know you had. They go into a whole thing about how you can find space in your attic for a whole new room when you're expecting a new baby.

I live in an apartment house. I don't have an attic. I'd like a suggestion on how to find space in my closet for a new pair of shoes. Most of the time I have to throw out an old pair to make room for the new pair. The fellow with the attic doesn't have my problem. He can keep adding all the new babies he wants without throwing out even one old one.

What's more, he can go to the bank for a home-improvement loan to make room for the new baby. If I went to the bank to ask for a home-improvement loan to make room for a new pair of shoes, they'd think I'm some kind of nut. I don't have to tell you . . . nobody gives a home-improvement loan to a nut.

Another suggestion you find in these seventy-five-cent magazines is the use of decorative room dividers to divide your living room into a living room and dining area. That let's me out because from the size of the rooms in my apartment, the architect started with a living room and divided it up into a whole apartment including kitchen and bath.

At this point I realized that any magazine called *House and Garden* didn't apply to me. An apartment isn't a house and three potted plants aren't a garden. A foyer with three orange crates stacked high with the first and last editions of all the New York newspapers that have opened and folded in the last couple of years isn't going to bring a photographer from *House Beautiful.*

Obviously, solving my lack of space problems is penny-ante stuff. To be scorned by decorating editors who direct their remarks to people who paper their walls, lambrequins and doors in the same floral print, and repeat this same floral motif in a pastel drawing over the bed, in the material of the bedspread and the fresh live flowers in the Sèvres vase by the bed.

Then a friend of mine who is also a city apartment house dweller who lacks storage space gave me an idea.

"Get a foot locker," she said. "Paint it the same color as your bedroom. It'll be a conversation piece. Nobody'll ever guess what it is."

So I went to an army navy surplus store, bought a foot locker and painted it blue. She was right about it being a conversation piece. Every ex-GI who sees it starts a conversation that goes, "Oh, you took a foot locker and painted it blue."

That's where I store my World War II meat-ration card. Also, half a parachute with a dress pattern given to me by a WAC who lost interest in the whole thing as soon as she was out of uniform.

Taxing Taxes

Just as I pay my taxes, Governor Rockefeller comes out with new announcements about new taxes.

Once he announced an increase in taxes without

mentioning what the new taxable items were going to be.

How could he? He's trying to come up with items that aren't taxed already.

I can't think of any. He must be having the same trouble.

I don't have any objections to paying taxes because if you don't make it, you don't have it and you don't pay taxes.

Except that with what Governor Rockefeller has in mind about tax increases, you'll be making it, paying taxes and then not have it.

How come the war on poverty suddenly turned into the war for poverty?

I'd like to know where the Governor thinks we're going to get the money to pay more taxes. He's asking us for more money like we're all Rockefellers.

With all his money, what does he need me for?

If he were a real sport, he'd bring a little from home and I'd be off the hook.

To tell you the truth, when I voted for Governor Rockefeller, it never occurred to me that a rich fellow like that would ask me to go Dutch treat.

❧ Danger—Kitchen

I don't know why everybody is so worried about the violence on television shows.

I'm worried about the violence on television commercials.

What cattleman way out in Wyoming, watching Bonanza, is going to be incited to violence against me for the water I use to keep a couple of potted plants going on my window sill?

I don't care how many Westerns he watches where the cattle ranchers force homesteaders off their land with violence. He's not going to saddle up and ride out to get me and my begonias.

It's the giant in my washer that's got me locking my bedroom door nights. There's something psychologically wrong about a giant using a washing machine for an orgone box.

How do I know he won't blow his top and pull me in with the wash? When I'm alone in the house I never do my laundry unless I'm armed. What's more I never turn my back on the washing machine when I'm sorting my laundry either. Who wants to be remembered for being whiter than white?

Weather forecasts mean nothing if you're planning to wash your kitchen floor. Dr. Frank Field assures you it's safe to go out in your small craft on the wide sea but in my kitchen, I'm in danger of being blown to kingdom come by a white tornado if I so much as dip a mop into a pail of floor cleaner.

According to the TV commercials for cleaning aids, Cape Kennedy is Disneyland compared to the energy stored in my stove cleaner, not to mention the power released in water by the cleaner I use for big jobs.

Who cares how gentle this stuff is to my hands? It's what happens to the rest of me that I'm worried about.

I have an arsenal of destruction in the soaps and powders under my sink. These weapons in the hands of our enemies could wipe us clean off the face of the earth. Really clean!

I never let a cleaning woman into my house without a security check taken personally by J. Edgar Hoover. It seems to me that the big arms experts aren't at the Pentagon in Washington. The fellows we should be consulting are at Procter and Gamble in Cincinnati.

Maybe Red China hasn't got the bomb. That big boom could have been suds clog.

Is There A Little Mad Scientist In Your Home?

I like to browse around in toy stores. Why not? I'm an adult and I can do anything I want to do.

And from the toys I see for children, I see that they can do anything they want to do too.

There are an awful lot of toys for little boys that are miniature replicas of what Daddy uses.

I saw a small "Do-It-Yourself Carpentry Kit" just like Daddy's big one so that a little boy can cut his little finger just like Daddy cuts his big finger.

I saw a miniature safety razor that was an exact scale model of Daddy's. Now really, do you know any three-year-olds who shave? Or even a nine-year-old? Well, maybe a nine-year-old, but not many.

I saw something called "The Headshrinker's Kit." At first I thought that it might be the old-fashioned "Doctor's Kit" brought up to date so that the kid could play at being a psychiatrist. But on examining it I discovered that there was no couch, no box of kleenex, no tranquilizers and not even a small plastic unconscious.

This was really a headshrinker's working outfit to shrink heads, including a few heads to practice on.

What happens when the kid uses up these practice heads and becomes a headshrinking enthusiast?

I remember when I was a small girl, my mother bought me a sewing kit. It came complete with needles and thread and small scraps of material to sew on. I threaded and sewed, became enthusiastic about sewing and used up all the material that came with the sewing kit. I went to my mother and she found some spare needles and thread and small scraps of material so that I could continue my new enthusiasm.

When the little headshrinking enthusiast goes to his mother, how is she going to come up with a spare head?

There are very few two-headed mothers. And with all the permissiveness around there are liable to be a lot less one-headed mothers.

And those games that come under the heading of educational toys read like army-training films.

Little boys can now put missiles together, make their own spaceships and load them.

What's going on here? The grown-up world is concentrating on a test ban and the kids are having an arms race. From the way they're going at it, it's each Mouseketeer for himself.

What good is that hot line between Washington and Moscow? What we need is a hot line between Washington and the Little Leaguers.

We could get up some morning and find that some little fat shortstop rules the world.

How about the day when mother's power-mad little scientist is so caught up with his toys that he won't do his homework anymore and won't practice the violin?

What happens when his mother threatens to take away his toys? He could turn her in to the FBI for being subversive.

Suppose this little Benedict Arnold has sold out to the other side. Is it nice for a little boy to say to his mother, "WE WILL BURY YOU"?

The only moment of happiness contemplating a future of small boys building spaceships to take them to the moon is that there is not one hint in any of their instructions as to how they'll get back.

I Never Met A Kid
I Didn't Like

I was brought up to have respect for my elders. On my own I have developed respect for my youngers.

Kids are really smarter than anybody. It's a shame we all grow up to be dumb adults.

Any time I have spent with children has been a ball, which is more than I can say about the time I have spent with their parents. And which is more than their parents can say about the time they spent with me.

A friend of mine, whom I hadn't seen in years, moved into the neighborhood.

While she was getting settled, I offered to take her small daughter. Since I had never met little Amy before, I fixed her some ice cream to establish a friendly relationship.

Now she looks at the plate of ice cream and says, "If I eat the ice cream are you going to ask me questions?"

So I said, "What do you mean, questions? Questions about what?"

Still leaving the ice cream untouched, she says, "You know!"

I said, "No, I don't know. What do you mean?"

So she says, "Well, where we used to live, the woman who lived next door to us called me into her apartment, gave me ice cream and asked me questions about the fight my mother and father had. When I got home and told my mother she was so mad and did I get it!"

Still leaving the ice cream uneaten, she continued, "So now I'm only allowed to answer certain questions," she said.

"Eat your ice cream," I said. "I'm not going to ask you any questions."

"Well," she says, "you can ask me how old I am, where I go to school, what class I'm in, if I like school and what I'm going to be when I grow up. If I answer any other questions my mother says I'm going to be punished."

"Eat your ice cream," I said. "It's melting."

Amy starts eating the ice cream and suddenly stops and says to me, "You know what the fight my mother and father had was about? My father had lunch with his first wife and didn't tell my mother about it. The way she found out . . ."

"Wait a minute," I interrupted her. "Didn't you tell me you'd be punished for doing exactly what you're doing now?"

"Nothing is going to happen to me," she said, "because I've already been punished for telling this."

I once took Amy and her little friend Georgia over to the Ed Sullivan rehearsal so they could meet Topo Gigio, the Italian mouse, whom I happen to know personally. As a matter of fact, I write his material when he appears on the Sullivan show.

You think it's odd to be writing for a mouse? What about Ed Sullivan? He stands there and talks to him. And from Topo Gigio's popularity in this country, you must all be sitting in front of your television sets listening.

Walking over to the TV studio, Georgia kept telling us about her divorced mother's new boy friend. She kept on about the presents she was getting every time he came over to see her mother. And besides new dolls and games and even dresses, he planned Sunday outings with her mother which included Georgia.

I could see that little Georgia was primed to the peak of acceptance when she said to Amy, "I never got so many presents. It's like every day is Christmas."

Amy, who had run this course when her mother remarried listened quietly. Then Georgia said, "I wish Mummie would marry him."

And Amy said, "Goodbye Christmas!"

It was a little while after this that Amy's mother went to the hospital to have her second child. Since Amy's stepfather was in the hospital with her mother I offered to take Amy until her grandmother picked her up later in the evening.

It was close to dinnertime so I started fixing dinner for both of us.

When we sat down to eat I poured myself a glass of beer. When Amy saw this she said, "Can I taste that?"

So I let her taste it. She tasted the beer, made an awful face and I was off the hook.

When I lit a cigarette she again said, "Can I taste that?"

I let her taste it. I figured if I said no she might feel unhappy and frustrated and besides with a new baby in the house there was going to be an awful lot of "no" to her, so why should I give her any trouble.

She tasted the cigarette, made an awful face and again I was off the hook.

While we were at the table eating, she suddenly looked at me and said, "Miss Diamond, do you know where babies come from?"

Of course I know where babies come from but I'm not going to tell her. I don't know if her mother read Dr. Spock or has been coasting along on that snow job about buying babies in Macy's basement.

So I did the sneaky thing.

I said, "Do you know where babies come from?"

And you know, she did. This kid started talking and it was like listening to Dr. Joyce Brothers.

Right in the middle of this elementary but factual account my telephone rang. It was Amy's stepfather.

As I handed her the phone he obviously was asking her if she was all right and what she was doing.

And Amy said, "Smoking, drinking and I'm telling Miss Diamond where babies come from!"

When the new baby was brought home, in order to thwart any attempts on his life, which is quite normal on the part of children who have been an "only child," Amy was given an important new status in the family. She was now "mother's big girl."

She was given twenty-five cents a week to spend any way she liked in Woolworth's. She was permitted to use catsup in whatever amount and on whatever foods she chose. She was also permitted to use her mother's hair spray.

However, mother's big girl's television-viewing hours were not extended nor was her bedtime.

So every night she balked at going to bed at 8:30 just as she did before she was "mother's big girl."

As a matter of fact, she began to have doubts about really being "mother's big girl."

This particular night she really raised a rumpus about not being allowed to stay up to watch Merv Griffin. She cried, rolled herself up into a ball under the bed and directed threats at the baby. The least of which were drowning and throwing him into The Time Tunnel.

Her mother, who had done a considerable amount of reading on sibling rivalry said to her, "Tears, tantrums —I can't believe you're 'mother's big girl.'"

And Amy said, "I can't either and neither would Merv Griffin!"

When Amy's mother told me about this I decided to tell Merv about it the next time I was on his show.

Since I would mention Amy's name, her mother gave her permission to stay up and hear it. Which she did.

The next day when I saw Amy she said to me, "You're not a writer. You're a repeater."

And she's so right. I often repeat the time I was on my way to the West Coast. Amy and her mother drove with me to the airport.

Amy kept asking me how high up I was going to be flying in the plane.

I told her the plane would fly way up into the sky until she couldn't see it at all and it would fly even higher in the sky and way up above the clouds.

"Isn't that where heaven is?" she asked me.

"Just about," I said.

And Amy said, "While you're up there, say hello to God!"

Joe Garagiola was telling me how his work traveling with the team, broadcasting on NBC Monitor and doing television sport shows keeps him away from home a great deal. As a result of all this, his small daughter sees him more often on television than she sees him around the house.

One day Joe came home unexpectedly. His wife called to their daughter who was playing in another room.

"Come see Daddy," she called out.

Running in, the kid said, "On what channel?"

When Sid Caesar's daughter, now a young matron, was quite small she suddenly asked one day, "Daddy, what's your name?"

He said, "Sid."

Then she said, "What does mummie call you?"

He said, "Sid."

She thought for a while and then she said, "What's your other name?"

"It's Caesar, like your other name," Sid said.

She thought a little longer this time and then pointing a wiggly finger at him, she said in a voice not completely believing, "You're Sid Caesar!"

🐟 Miracle On A
Crosstown Bus

I would no sooner get on a bus with a five-dollar bill than I would throw myself under a bus. Either way you're taking your life in your hands.

So before I get on a bus, I carefully choose the smallest change I have or at most a one-dollar bill.

Well, one day I got on a crowded bus and much to my horror discovered that all I had in my purse was a five-dollar bill.

The bus started to move. I was doomed. My whole life passed before my eyes.

The first fellow I ever kissed and all the fellows before him I should have.

The three No. 1 eraser-tipped lead pencils I filched from NBC.

The time I put on all that weight and accused the dry cleaner of shrinking my clothes.

It was ghastly.

I faced the bus driver and chanced it. My Blue Cross is always paid up. I handed him the five-dollar bill and started the countdown because the bus driver was going to send me to the moon.

He took the five-dollar bill.

Here it comes, I thought. Vengeance is his. Since he made no attempt to do me bodily harm I figured he's going to get even with me another way. He's going to give me my change in pennies and I'll just have to stand there while he counts them out.

Nothing happened. He didn't say anything at all and gave me my change quite normally.

Now if this were Christmas, I could accept it as part of the season of miracles. But there were still 116 shopping days left until Christmas.

I don't think I have ever experienced anything more inspirational than this bus driver forgiving me the sin of getting on a bus to pay the fare with a five-dollar bill.

I'm sure he can drive that bus on water.